# The Well Socialized Dog:
## Step-by-Step Socialization Training
## For Puppies and Dogs

## By Faye Dunningham

ISBN-13: 978-1479173372

A B C Chags Publishing

# Table of Contents

What Proper Socialization Means ............................1

Your Dog's Changing Personality ...........................6

Inherent Canine Instinct .......................................9

The Size of Your Puppy's World ...........................13

A Tiny World .........................................................15

Just a Bit Larger .....................................................16

What Size Will You Choose? .................................19

Home Socialization – How to Build the Perfect
Foundation ...............................................................22

Why Socialization Should Begin at Home .......24

The Importance of Touch .....................................27

The Importance of Voice ......................................29

Your Property – Finding Out What Your Puppy
Needs to Be Socialized To ....................................31

Socializing Your Puppy or Dog with Visitors to
Your Home ................................................................35

Strangers, Dogs and Other Triggers – Teaching
Your Puppy to be Well Behaved No Matter
Where You Go ...........................................................53

The Process for Meet and Greets with Strangers 55

Making a Decision about a Meet and Greet ....62

The Process for Meet and Greets with Other Dogs ..................................................................................68

The "Canine Hello" .............................................69
First, Meet the Neighbor Dogs and Friends' Dogs....................................................................71
Encountering Unknown "Stranger" Dogs.......78
Helping Your Dog Tolerate Traffic......................81

Introduction to Traffic .........................................82
Troubleshooting - If Your Dog Barks at Traffic ..................................................................................85
Troubleshooting - If Your Dog is Afraid of Traffic .................................................................87
Other Pets – Creating a Home of Peace, Happiness and Friendship.....................................94

Testing for Possible Friendship ..........................96
Helping Your Puppy Be Comfortable with Another Pet...........................................................97
Your Dog as a Passenger in the Car – It Needn't be a Nightmare .......................................................104

If Your Puppy is Afraid of the Car...................105
Canine Car Sickness ...........................................110
Your Dog and Your New Baby .............................112

Before Your Baby Arrives ..................................114
Your Baby's Toys and Your Dog's Toys .........119
Only a Certain Amount of Time ......................120

After the Baby Arrives ........................................ 122

Thunderstorm Training ........................................ 124

Is This Normal Behavior? .................................. 127

How to Help ....................................................... 127

Air Pressure ....................................................... 130

Exploring and Expanding Your Dog's World ... 133

Places to Ponder ................................................ 133

There is No Limit ............................................... 138

# Preface

Just about every owner has heard of the term "socialization" but can rarely find detailed instructions on what is it that they are supposed to do and specifically how to do it. This book is your answer. Great time has been taken to create this guide which will lead you through every step of socializing your puppy or dog.

Your puppy or dog will never learn socialization on his own; he needs your loving guidance. It will be your job (and a fun one at that!) to not only introduce him to the world and all it holds, but how to properly interact with it as well.

The difference between a socialized dog and one that is improperly socialized (or has a complete lack of socialization) is colossal. A well socialized dog will be a self-confident dog. This, in turn, gives you a well-behaved dog!

Dogs that lack proper socialization are much more prone to barking issues, behavioral issues and often do not follow commands as they otherwise would. A dog may bark erratically, act out with destructive behavior, display aggressiveness or become nervous or shy in a variety of situations without having been properly socialized.

After following along with the detailed steps in this book, you will find that you have a dog that carries himself with enough confidence to handle any situation and will make you proud by being well mannered in all types of settings. Best of all, a well socialized dog is a happy dog, and the end result will be a content canine companion, which is what all loving owners want.

Enjoy your read!

# What Proper Socialization Means

This book will be going into great detail regarding socializing your puppy or dog to the world. Chances are that you have a puppy right now. Some of you will have an older dog...A dog that you perhaps rescued or adopted...And that older dog was never socialized as he or she should have been.

For the owner of a dog of any age at all, this book will guide you through all of the necessary steps of socialization. We will talk about why certain things should be done and then specifically how to do them. We will go over how to handle a puppy that has already developed a negative reaction to something...And also how to introduce a puppy to a new element.

Since the large majority of you who will be reading this book are owners of puppies, we will use the word "puppy" throughout this book.  If you have an older dog that is in need of proper socialization that he or she never lovingly received earlier by a previous owner, all of the following will still apply even though the word "puppy" will be used. After all, a ten year old dog that was never introduced to the many elements of the world *is* in a sense still a puppy….As many things will be new to him or her!

You probably have heard of the term "socialization" but what does this really mean? Can it happen just by living day to day as you normally would?  Does it come naturally or do you have to purposefully socialize your puppy?

While a puppy will *naturally* come into contact with elements in his day to day living, a puppy *will* need your guidance when encountering *many* of them. Socialization is the method of *directing* that introduction between your puppy and various elements in his world.  It *not only* includes the introduction of things, it *also* involves teaching your puppy the proper response to the input that he is receiving.

An *introduction* to a new element, (a person, a place, a situation, another animal, etc.) offers a puppy the opportunity of discovery; to see something new, to hear something new. If the introduction is fleeting, the puppy will process and store that limited information. This type of partial and restricted socialization can happen throughout a normal day without any purposeful contribution by you.

*However*, proper socialization will involve teaching your puppy how to go beyond introduction and to actually interact with the element (*if* there should even be a desired interaction). *Additionally*, it will involve teaching your puppy *how* that element should be perceived and how the puppy should react to it. Should he stay away (electrical cord)? Should he have no fear (a family friend)? Should he learn to tolerate it (cars driving by)?

Without your guidance, your puppy can become extremely overwhelmed with his world. It will be your job to properly socialize him to each and every element *that is worthy of an emotional and/or physical response.*

There are many things to socialize your puppy to that *are* worthy of dictating an emotional or physical response. This includes people (friends, acquaintances and strangers), other dogs (both those known and unknown), and other animals. It will encompass situations such as being at the park, walking down a street next to busy traffic and going to the veterinarian. It will include becoming accustomed to walking on different surfaces such as sand and snow. And it will also include being familiarized with noises such as car alarms, thunder storms and even crying babies.

On the other hand, there are many things that do not warrant attention. Those will be the elements that a puppy needs no guidance with and will simply accept as "part of life". These are inconsequential things such as a television show playing in the living room, the washing machine making noises and lights being turned off and on; a puppy will learn about those things as he goes about his day. Those trivial noises and situations will be assimilated into his mind without concern.

Without your guidance, a puppy can become very fearful of things such as car rides…Being picked up and touched by the veterinarian and so much more. Without your assistance, your puppy may be nervous and anxious around people who visit at your home….Or he may bark in response to seeing and hearing cars, other people or small animals.

A puppy may have a strong reaction to one element and seem oblivious to another; this often leaves an owner wondering "how" and "why". It may be a matter of a puppy not having received enough positive feedback when first encountering the element....Or it may simply be a matter of a puppy's particular personality and his or her capability to process a situation.

Each puppy will need varying levels of training to react and respond appropriately. Some puppies can become accustomed to an element in as little as one day...Others may need a much more gradual introduction over the course of several weeks or even a month.

Now that we understand what socialization is and why we must incorporate socialization training as we raise our puppy, we are going to discuss a very important window of time in a puppy's life.

# Your Dog's Changing Personality

There is a huge shift in the way that a puppy sees the world between the age of 8 weeks old and 12 to 16 weeks old. This 1 to 2 month window is one of great changes. Many owners do not know that this is normal and is part of the growing process, which can lead owners to not only become confused, it can cause them to not follow through with very much needed socialization training during this time.

Canine instinct dictates that a dog be wary of things, to be on guard for everything to be a possible threat unless proven otherwise. *This instinct often does not kick in until the age of 3 to 4 months old.* Before this time, a puppy is not able to properly process all of the data in the world around him. His mind picks up only bits and pieces. Those pieces of limited data are then processed with a low level of significance and stored away.

The owners of a new 8 week old puppy may often be happily surprised regarding how their puppy seems to be the friendliest puppy in the world...And that he or she adores everyone!  In many cases, this is a *temporary* display of behavior.

 As soon as that same puppy has the ability and the capacity to take in all that surrounds him, only *then* will he react to the *entire* weight of a situation.  And as previously mentioned this change often happens between the ages of 3 to 4 months old.

During the age of 8 weeks old to 12 to 16 weeks old, when the owner thought that the puppy was behaving fantastic in all situations, he or she mistakenly thought that this meant that the puppy did not need socialization.

If this is what has happened to you and your puppy, do not despair. While it would be best for socialization to start at the age of 8 weeks old (and even younger, if done by the breeder), it is never too late to begin. If your puppy is 3, 4, 5 months old or even older, socialization will have a great effect on him since he is now old enough to process and comprehend the stimuli that surrounds him.

Owners often become confused and wonder how their "normally" outgoing, friendly puppy changed into a nervous, nipping or excessively barking puppy. The important thing to remember is that the previous friendly behavior seen at the young age of 8 weeks old was not the all-inclusive *final* personality of the puppy. Being very young, the puppy did not have full awareness. This in turn only allowed him to absorb a limited amount of information. And therefore he did not have a complete and genuine behavioral response.

As your puppy grows, his personality will change. It is much like how humans will have changing personalities as they grow older throughout the years…But it happens at a very different rate of speed. The old notion that dog ages 7 years for each human year is just that: old. It is old and very untrue. The aging process, and therefore the maturing process of a dog, will be very fast during some phases of his life and slower during others.

Each dog breed grows and matures at his own particular rate of speed. Typically, toy and small breed dogs mature faster. Medium and large breed dogs mature slower. For example, during the first human year of 365 days, a toy breed such as a Pomeranian, Shih Tzu, Maltese, Yorkshire Terrier or Chihuahua will mature the equivalent of 15 human years. This means that by the age of 1 year old, a toy breed dog will be the equivalent of a young teenage human.

Alternatively, a large breed dog such as the Boxer or Akita will not reach the maturity level equivalent to a 15 year old human teenager until the age of 3 years old; it will take a much longer amount of time.

Once that age is met, (between the age of 1 to 3 years old depending on what breed of dog you have), growth and maturity levels develop at a much slower rate of speed as the dog matures from teenager to adult and finally to senior.

## Inherent Canine Instinct

As we talked about earlier, an 8 week old puppy may not even notice or seem to care that a person unknown to him has entered your home. His young mind is not yet able have a full grasp and realization that a stranger is an element that warrants attention.

He will often go about his business, playing with a toy or chewing on a treat. During this brief phase of development, when a puppy is active yet not quite aware of everything, he or she could be picked up by twenty strangers and not have any emotions of fear.

At this young age, most puppies understand that touch equals comfort; they have learned this from the dam (their mother). It is sad that some puppies lose this lesson if they are neglected...That instinct to feel safe and secure from touch can turn to fear of touch. But when they are nurtured and the lesson that touches are comforting is reminded, they will continue on to interpret this correctly.

If you take that 8 week old puppy (that seemed to have no fear) and jump ahead 1 month and see him as a 3 month old puppy, things are much different. The puppy is much more aware of his surroundings now, he has established what his territory (your home) is and he understands that certain new noises and the linked voices to them equal another human entering into his world.

Now seeing a situation in its entirety, he can then (guided by raw canine instinct) have a more profound reaction. ....If no socialization has been done (or limited or inadequate socialization has been attempted), many times "flight or fight" occurs...He *may* fight (stand in a guarded position and/or bark) *or* the *flight* instinct may kick in (running into another room, cowering down on the floor, trying to get you to pick him up, etc.)

Can you imagine if humans had to live this way? Imagine if no one ever told you that the mail carrier was a friendly person and not a threat and your instinct told you to be on guard…To this day, you would become very nervous whenever he approached your property to drop off your mail.

Your instinct would tell you that *perhaps* he is a danger. You not only could not relax while the mail carrier was outside of you home,  you would also become nervous in *anticipation* of him coming….And *after* he left, part of you would worry that he was going to return. This is how a puppy feels if not socialized to elements that trigger a reaction.

So we have now learned that it is normal for a puppy's personality to change. We know that a puppy that previously showed no fear may begin to be wary of certain things.  We also understand that socialization training should begin at the age of 8 weeks old even if a puppy is reacting to all situations just fine.

Last but not least, proper socialization can be taught to a puppy or dog of any age. In the next chapter, we will discuss how it is you who literally controls the size of your puppy's world and why this is of great importance.

# The Size of Your Puppy's World

The size of your puppy's world will be the size that you allow it to be. Remember this. It is of great value and worth repeating to yourself many times.

I once rescued a tiny Pomeranian; she had been forced to live in one room for almost a decade. The room was carpeted and she went to the bathroom in that room wherever she stood at the time of needing to urinate or eliminate, since she was never brought outside a day in her life.

At the approximate age of ten, she did not know what it felt like to have soft green grass under her tiny paws. She did not know that stairs existed. She did not know what a leash was.

When I cuddled her in my arms and took her away from that awful tiny world that she had lived in for a decade, I had an enormous sense of joy that filled my heart. I felt extremely honored that I was going to be able to give this enchanting dog a much larger world, while keeping her safe and secure.

The responsibility of socializing her to the world was not a burden. It was an uplifting, magnificent mission. Your job to socialize your puppy should be looked at in the same way. It is a great responsibility but it is also a great honor to socialize a puppy.

You have complete control over the size of his world. Hopefully you will allow it to be a big world...A world that holds interesting elements and one that offers the joy of discovery. When done correctly, socialization will give your puppy self-confidence. It will allow him to have the confidence to discover and to learn.

A fearful, nervous dog is not a happy dog. A dog that jumps at every noise and barks at every movement is living a life of *near constant stress*. Even if a dog is not socialized to just *one* element....let's say the element of cars driving by...This places him in a stressful situation *daily*. It will affect him when brought outside for bathroom needs, when going for walks and perhaps even when looking out of a window.

## A Tiny World

Let's look at what the size of your puppy's world was right up until the time that you brought him home...And then we will talk about what size is best for it to become.

When a puppy is born, his world is very tiny. It is usually the size of a 4x6 foot cardboard box or playpen. He does not know that anything exists outside of this 4x6 foot world of his for the first few weeks. Until the beginning of week three, even the owner will not be perceived as much more than a distinct type of touch. The puppy's eyes will remain closed and the puppy will not be able to fully hear.

So, during these first couple of weeks, he only knows of his tiny world by touch. He understands the touch of his littermates and the soft comfort of snuggling close to the dam.

Week three brings about a lot of changes. It is perhaps the most rapid week of changes for any dog. By the end of week three, eyes are open, hearing is almost at full capacity and the puppy is quickly learning to walk. Many owners do not think a lot about the element of a puppy learning to walk...But it is an amazing time of development. Within the time span of approximately one week, a puppy will progress from a wobbly little creature to one that can walk, trot and soon run.

## Just a Bit Larger

At the end of week three, a puppy's world has expanded just a tiny bit. It extends out just a bit further than the 4x6 foot box. The puppy is now aware of the human who is watching over him. He can sense her, see her and hear her. It would be wonderful if all owners and breeders took great care in socialization at this very young and impressionable age, but sadly many do not. Unfortunately, many puppies at this young age are left in a small box with very little human contact.

You may never be fully aware of how much socialization was given to a puppy before you obtained him. Despite any assurances that a puppy was "socialized", in many cases even a loving breeder does not have time to socialize each puppy in a litter to all of the possible elements that can trigger an inappropriate response.

Therefore, if the litter was kept in a playpen that was located next to a washing machine, the puppy may be accustomed to that noise. If the litter was kept in a living room that was located close to the front door…And the house had a lot of visitors, the puppy may be used to hearing the doorbell ring.

Being familiarized to these elements will be a good *foundation*; however the elements may need to reintroduced once the puppy is more aware. As we discussed earlier, puppies 3 to 4 months old and under have a limited ability to comprehend the entirety of a situation and will not show reaction that would normally occur if *full* awareness existed.

In many cases, when a litter of puppies reaches the age of 5, 6 and 7 weeks old, they are allowed to roam from the dam. They no longer need her constant warmth, nor do they need near constant nursing. Once sleeping up to 22 hours per day, a 5, 6 or 7 week old puppy will be awake for longer periods of time. While he will still nap quite a bit in comparison to an adult dog, he may sleep 18 to 20 hours per day as opposed to the previous 22 hours.

This gives a puppy more time to explore. The ability to have good control over motor skills allows a puppy to not just walk, but to run. Previously being confined to the box or playpen, his muscles are aching to be stretched.

Therefore, when raised correctly, from the age of 5 to 7 weeks a puppy learns that a world exists outside of his box. He can now see an entire room and can explore all of the objects in it. In most cases (aside from horrible puppy mills), a litter will be allowed to leave the dam and walk around and play in a certain room. When set up properly, that room will have been puppy-proofed so that there are no objects that can be broken and no objects that can be accidentally swallowed.

What an exciting time for a puppy! His entire world is just one room, but he is having such fun as he learns about dog toys and obstacles to climb over. He spends a lot of time wrestling with his littermates.

When raised correctly, by the age of 6 to 7 weeks, a puppy will be allowed outside, weather permitting, into a safe enclosed area. This expands his world a bit more. Even if the area would be perceived as "empty" to a person, a puppy will be filled with curiosity. He instinctually knows that the air quality is different; the concept of "indoors" and "outdoors" will be learned. He will smell new scents and hear new noises (birds chirping, airplanes flying overhead, etc.)

In some sad cases, a breeder will put puppies outside onto a cement surface with nothing to touch but a chain link fence that surrounds it. For these puppies, the feel of grass will need to be learned. Therefore, without being in the breeder's home for the first 2 months of a puppy's life, an owner will never know if the puppy's world was expanded in the way as described or if it was more limited. Do take joy in the fact that if you obtained your puppy from a reputable breeder, chances are that your puppy did indeed experience a comfortable, gradually expanding world.

In any case, once your puppy comes home to you it's a "whole new ballgame!" Life begins anew! Now, *you* are in complete control over the size of your puppy's world.

## What Size Will You Choose?

As mentioned earlier, the size of your puppy's world is completely up to you.

If your puppy was never taken off of your property unless taking him for veterinarian checkups, the puppy's world would be rather small. It would consist of the rooms in your home that the puppy had access to and the surrounding yard outside that he was brought out to for bathroom needs, play, etc. Interaction with humans and other animals would be limited to only those who lived in or visited the house.

If you took your puppy for daily walks, his world would expand to include the neighborhood. If the route was varied, heading south one day and then north on alternating days, it would expand the puppy's world even more by adding in *two* neighboring areas. The opportunities to encounter and be shown how to properly interact with people and other dogs would increase.

## Why You Should Make Your Puppy's World as Large as Possible

Aside from the discussed basics of bathroom needs and daily walks, if you bring your puppy to all sorts of locations, you can enlarge his world to include all types of wonderful experiences. Each experience and each location will at first bring about the opportunity to learn socialization skills. Then, with time, once a puppy is properly socialized, attention can be given to exploration and enjoyment of the environment.

When your puppy is accustomed to all different kinds of people, noises, animals and locations he will have a great amount of confidence. Once properly socialized, a puppy (soon to be an adult dog) will have no fears, no anxiety, and no nervousness.

Not one loving owner would intentionally place the emotions of fear, anxiety and nervousness onto their dog....And therefore by expanding his world to be as big as possible and using proper socialization techniques while doing so, an owner is then *purposefully and decisively* helping to raise a content, happy and emotionally well-balanced dog.

When a dog is emotionally well-balanced, he is more prone to be well-behaved. When a dog leads a full life that meets his physical and emotional needs, this neither leaves room nor need to act out with negative behavior.

Now that we have talked about the importance of how big your puppy's world should be, we will continue on in the next chapter to discuss how to begin.

# Home Socialization – How to Build the Perfect Foundation

Owners of new puppies may be eager to bring their new puppy out into the world and as discussed earlier, it is extremely important to do so. However, one must keep in mind that a young puppy is not fully protected by vaccinations until he has had all of his "puppy shots".

When nursing from the dam, antibodies of protection are passed down to the pup. Vaccinations begin. There is a window of time in which the antibodies that were passed down from the dam are no longer present (or are at very low inadequate levels), but the vaccination antibodies are not yet abundant enough to offer full protection.

For this reason, owners of new puppies should keep their puppies at home until the full round of "puppy shots" is complete and then count out for 2 weeks after that.

Limiting socialization at this early age is actually a good thing. Why? The answer is because the world should not be introduced all at once. For proper socialization skills, a puppy needs the process of experiencing new things to be gradual. It brings to mind the old saying that one must walk before one runs. *Home socialization* will be more than adequate to be the foundation for further skill building until a puppy's vaccinations are complete and the puppy is protected from disease.

A puppy will do much better with a group of dogs when first allowed to become used to playing with one dog. A puppy will behave better when you have a group of friends over to your home if he is first allowed to become used to one guest entering into the home. And so it goes on…

Most of the following training will be comprised of gradual increments of socialization. It will prevent stress to the puppy and while the process is gradual, it is the fastest route to success. To rush things is counterproductive, and you and your puppy may move backward instead of forward.

## Why Socialization Should Begin at Home

As we just discussed, a young puppy cannot be thrown into situations that are new, he must be allowed to take small steps. If an owner tries to force a puppy into a situation too quickly, before that puppy has gained self-confidence on smaller levels with less intense situations, it can cause a great deal of stress. In worst case situations, it can cause the puppy to have a phobia of the very thing that the owner tried to force the puppy to be socialized to.

Your home offers an array of socialization opportunities. There is so much for a puppy to learn about; however it should be done in increments. When first bringing a puppy home, owners are often so excited and happy that they do not realize just how overwhelming it can be for a puppy.

If a puppy is overwhelmed, it can cause stress. When a puppy undergoes stress it can cause hypoglycemia. Hypoglycemia is a term that is used to describe a rapid drop in blood sugar levels. Aside from stress, other elements can bring this on as well. Particularly with very tiny puppies, going too long without food can trigger this.

Since this is a serious condition and it can be fatal, all owners should be aware of the signs. Symptoms generally come on quickly and often progress very fast.

Signs that indicate this include: Sudden weakness (your puppy may appear to go "weak in the knees" and/or appear to have trouble standing), dizziness (your puppy may walk into a wall or other object that he would normally avoid or go around), and sleepiness (while it is normal for a puppy to become sleepy and take a lot of naps, this type of sudden sleepiness will be pronounced and abrupt).

One highly recommended method to treat this as you are preparing to bring your puppy to the closest animal hospital or veterinarian's office is to rub some honey onto the puppy's gums. Many informational sources will list Karo syrup as a substance to use, however it acts as a laxative and this can cause even more problems.

When honey is rubbed into the gums, it is absorbed directly into the blood stream and it may help to stabilize a puppy as he is being brought to a veterinarian for treatment. For this reason, it is recommended to always have honey on hand. After the honey is given, the puppy must be brought to the veterinarian ASAP so that blood sugar levels can be monitored as additional treatment is often needed.

With this in mind, while this will be a time of happiness and excitement, it is highly suggested to keep things a "family affair" for the first week or so. If a new puppy is only introduced to his immediate human family members, it will allow him to gain his bearings before moving on to meeting other people.

A new puppy should be allowed to explore the home at a pace of his own choosing. The puppy should not be required to run from room to room. Simply allow your puppy to go into any room that he wishes, as long as you have "puppy-proofed" it first for potential dangers.

 **It is extremely important to "puppy-proof" all rooms and areas that a puppy will have access to, even if for a brief period of time. Absolutely anything that *can* fit into your puppy's mouth should be looked at as if your puppy *will* mouth it! All small items should be picked up, not only from the floor but also from any area that a puppy could potentially reach (imagine your puppy standing on his hind legs).**

**While you may feel that your puppy will never have the urge to chew on electrical cords...Or if you "know" that you will always have an eye on your puppy to stop him from attempting to do so, it will still be important to secure all cords away from your puppy's reach. It only takes a moment for an**

**owner to turn away and for a puppy to find a cord and bite down in an endeavor to discover, "What is this?"**

Within the first hour of arrival, the puppy should be shown where his food and water bowl is located. His food and water area should remain in one location. To a puppy, food means survival. His canine instinct sends a strong and unavoidable message that his very life depends on ingesting food and drinking water. Make sure to choose one certain spot for the puppy's bowls and take care to always make sure that the food and water is fresh. This will help keep a puppy feeling at ease.

If you have a large family and especially if you have several children, everyone may want to play with, cuddle and pick up the puppy. It is best to allow everyone to take turns, *with breaks in between*, as to not overwhelm him.

## The Importance of Touch

It cannot be overstated how important touch is. When a puppy is not handled enough it can cause him to never be able to have tolerance for grooming (bathing, brushing, nail trimming, ear cleaning, dental care, wiping of the eyes). Without handling, he will often not, on his own, be the type of dog that cuddles up next to you on the sofa. The aloof adult dog that avoids close interaction with his humans is the grown-up version of the puppy that was not generously touched and handled.

Therefore, touching and handling your puppy is a part of socialization. Most dogs without "touch socialization" are very impatient when their paws are handled....when an owner is attempting to trim nails...when an owner is attempting to locate a sliver and a host of other random reasons to handle the dog over the course of a life time.

Dogs also often show great reluctance to having their teeth brushed if they are not routinely desensitized to having their teeth and mouth touched.

An owner should establish a firm precedence that the puppy is to hold still whenever his human is handling him. Your goal is to make it such an ordinary occurrence that should you need to check your dog for an attached tick or you need to grab a non-food possible choking object from his mouth, that he sits still and allows you to do it.

Begin with small steps, simply holding your puppy and patting him. Touch the tail, the ears, and the paws. As we discussed earlier on, a young puppy that is 8 weeks old and up to 16 weeks old can be easily distracted and not fully aware of all that is happening. It is during this age that desensitizing him to being handled works best.

As you do this each day, he will be becoming more aware and the 2 elements will blend seamlessly together; giving you a puppy and then adult dog that does not run away from bath time or try to escape a grooming session.

Best done at an early age, but able to be done with even a ten year old dog, an owner should gently open the puppy's mouth. Using a finger, all teeth should be touched: front, back and tops. This should be done for a couple of minutes each day. After a few weeks of this, regular brushings with canine toothpaste and toothbrush should be tolerated.

## The Importance of Voice

The more that you (and any other human family members) speak to your puppy, the better it is. It does not matter that your puppy does not know what you are saying. It is the tone of your voice and the frequency of how often you speak directly to your puppy that is most important.

If you are feeling frustrated, it will come across in your tone, so it is best to refrain from speaking to your puppy if you are feeling upset or worried. Those feelings can be easily transferred from you onto him.

He is very capable of picking up on your tone. If you sound worried, a puppy will metaphorically think, "If my human is worried, maybe I should be worried too!" This can make a puppy nervous. He may whine and/or pace due to expecting something unpleasant to be just around the corner.

Your puppy will learn which tones are friendly and which are not. This will come in very handy when you are ready to socialize him to other people. The words that you say do not often matter.

For example, you can come home and say, "Work was so rough today, I am starving and the house is a big mess", but if said in a happy, enthusiastic tone your puppy will understand those words to mean, "I am happy, it is a wonderful day, life is good and you are a delightful dog!"

## Your Property – Finding Out What Your Puppy Needs to Be Socialized To

When you bring your puppy outside for his bathroom needs, once he has eliminated you should walk him around your property. Alternatively, you can choose another convenient time of the day. Allow him to stop along the way to investigate what he wishes as long as it is not harmful (chemically treated grass, fire ants, etc.) When young, he may not have yet experienced the scent of a certain flower before...and just that element can bring about the joy of discovery.

If the weather is pleasant, stay outside for a good

amount of time. Sit together and allow your puppy to see squirrels and hear the chirping of birds. If you live on a busy street, allow him to have short times of sitting on leash beside you to hear the cars driving by.

If it is raining, put on your raincoat and allow your puppy to become accustomed to the feel of the raindrops falling down upon him.

If it is snowing, bundle up (and bundle up your puppy – especially if you have a toy or small breed dog – with booties and a sweater) and allow him to become accustomed to seeing the snowflakes falling down and feel how the ground now feels solid as opposed to soft grass.

The *key* element in all of this is to take notice of which things your puppy easily accepts as "part of life". With those things, he will may act oblivious to the element....Or he may show curiosity, check things out and while you are saying "Good Boy" or "Good Girl" your puppy will then move on to the next element that catches his attention.

For *any* element that appears to cause nervous, anxious or wary behavior, the element should be "red flagged" as one that your puppy will need to be socialized to.

If you socialize your puppy to elements encountered while at home, you will have much better success when doing so with elements outside of the home and the property.

For example, let's take a look at what to do if your puppy acts frantic in the rain, appearing to have a strong dislike for feeling it falling upon him. While it may seem like a good idea to avoid the rain, this is the exactly what *not* to do. Avoidance of a trigger will reinforce the fear and never allow your puppy to be socialized to the element.

Therefore, you will mark this as a "red flag" that warrants socialization training. The goal will then be to introduce and teach interaction and reaction in slow, gradual steps.

Each time that it is raining will be an opportunity to do this training. You will want to remain calm while you plan to head out. Keep the time spent in the rain short: one to three minutes. Do not immediately bring him back inside. It will be important to NOT offer soothing words during these short, first initial explorations of an element that bothers your puppy.

If you say in a soothing voice, "It's okay, calm down, the rain is not going to hurt you"....It will send a message to your puppy that he is correct in being upset and that you, his leader, agrees since you are now trying to soothe him.

You will want to act in a very casual way. Just speak in a normal tone. You can say just about anything that you want, aside from "NO" or the soothing words of "It's okay", just say it in a matter-of-fact way. The goal is to show your puppy, by your words and your calm actions that the rain is of no bother to you.

Each time it does rain, make it a point to bring your puppy outside. *Each time you do this increase the time increment by 1 to 2 minutes.* Each time, act casual as described. Ignore any barking, begging, nudging against you or any other attention-seeking behavior.

As the session time is ending and you are ready to bring your puppy back inside, if your puppy is acting calm take that moment to offer a special treat and praise before entering back into the home.

When you do this on a regular basis, your puppy will learn that since you do not mind the rain (or traffic noises, or bird chirping, or snowfall or any other outside element) that neither should he. You will lead by example and he, ruled by canine instinct, will choose to follow your lead.

# Socializing Your Puppy or Dog with Visitors to Your Home

As explained earlier, a very young puppy may appear to be oblivious to guests in your home or even show very friendly behavior. As your puppy grows a bit older, he will have then learned that the home and the property is his "territory" and his canine instinct to protect the home will have grown much stronger.

On the flip side of protection mode, some puppies will become shy, and will then become nervous when others are around. Puppies that feel this way may constantly nudge at you for attention, shake in fear or try to hide.

Fortunately, there is one answer to the many ways that a puppy may negatively behave when guests arrive, since there is only one main trigger: The puppy is not desensitized to the element. Socialization training will work to fix that.

For a puppy, when a guest arrives, he now has a lot to think about. Not only may he feel an urge to protect, he may also additionally feel as if his territory is being invaded and encroached upon.

The thoughts that metaphorically run through a puppy's mind are, "Who is this person?" "Is this a friend or foe?" "Should I go into protection mode?" "Am I in danger and should I hide" "What is their intention?" "Does my human need my guard services?" Without the answers to these questions, a dog of any size, from a 4 pound Pomeranian to a 20 pound Boxer will have a mixture of these same thoughts.

It will be your job to show your puppy, by your words and by your actions that they have no reason to: be afraid, be on guard, be nervous, bark, or show any other behavior other than being relaxed and friendly.

If your puppy has been proven to show negative behavior with guests, do plan ahead with your visitors regarding the training that you are going to implement. It is best if they understand what you are doing as opposed to you having to try to explain yourself while also trying to focus on the socialization training.

The most common behaviors of a puppy that is not socialized to guests are: barking, jumping, hiding or nudging you for attention. There are other odd quirks that a puppy can have...Therefore, while your puppy may act out in his own particular way, we will use the words "negative behavior" to encompass whatever he is doing that is causing problems.

You may replace this with "nudge you" or "jump around" or "hide in fear", as ultimately the training for this aspect will be the same.

The first reactions that most owners have, when puppies are showing negative behavior, are to say "Shhhhhh", try to reprimand them or remove them from the room. None of those techniques will work.

Saying "Shhhhhh" is the same as offering a soothing message. As we learned in the previous chapter in the section of "Your Property – Finding Out What Your Puppy Needs to Be Socialized To"....offering any words in a tone that could be interpreted as soothing is the same as confirming that your puppy is correct in feeling afraid or disturbed.

Therefore, when owners say "Shhhhh", they are unknowingly encouraging the behavior.

If you try and reprimand him, it may cause a temporary pause in the negative behavior as you may be able to momentarily avert his attention, but it does not teach proper socialization skills.

If you remove your puppy from the room, this will be counterproductive. While you may gain the temporary relief being away from the negative behavior, you are removing any opportunity to implement socialization training. Your puppy will never move forward in his ability to control his actions. It will be become commonplace for him to be removed when a guest comes over and not only will this not stop negative behavior, but it often increases it.

Now that you understand what not to do and you will be sure to stop yourself from doing any of that, let's discuss what you *should* do.

Have a treat readily available in your pocket. Do not allow your puppy to see you place it there or have any idea that you have a hidden treat at all.

# The Treat

Let's pause for a moment to talk about the importance of the type of treat that must be used to stop any moderate to severe negative behavior when you are implementing socialization training with your puppy.

It must not be a "normal" treat. It must have great meaning. If a dog is routinely given the same type of small treat regularly throughout the day in addition to their meals, if it is then given to them as a reward, it will not actually be seen as a reward. To a dog, it will mean nothing more than "Oh, a bit of food, thank you".

Most puppies and dogs simply love bacon. Bacon is often declared to be off limits to humans who are trying to eat a healthy diet. However, many people do not know the actual nutritional value of one piece of bacon. When a piece of bacon is microwaved and then squeezed with a paper towel to soak up excess fat/grease, it is a healthy treat to give as a special reward when a person is working to train a dog in regard to a strong behavioral habit.

What works best is pre-cooked bacon which can be found under many brand names and is less expensive when obtained under a generic name. Unlike dog treats that are artificially flavored to taste like bacon, it has no fillers, no artificial coloring and no artificial flavors.

One piece of pre-cooked bacon which has been microwaved for 20 seconds and fat has been soaked up with a paper towel contains 15.5 calories. It contains 5 grams of protein. It contains 5 grams of fat (which is needed as part of any food plan, especially for puppies).

It is best when cooked well, allowed to cool and then crumbled. When done this way, one piece can be used for two reward times. In this way, each reward will contain only 7.75 calories.

You may wish to choose a different treat other than the above mentioned bacon and that is fine. The important element is that: Your dog simply loves the taste and it is not a treat that is normally given out. It is an extra delicious treat that is only given as a reward for good behavior.

## Back to the Training

Now that you are completely prepared with a special treat hidden in your pocket or close enough to you that you can easily grab it, it is time to continue on.

The key is to completely ignore the negative behavior. You may at first think that this is the same as approving it. It is not. Ignoring negative behavior, when done properly, sends out a strong message that the negative behavior does not warrant your attention what-so-ever. As your dog's leader, your puppy will learn (after a few lessons) that if you do not think that the negative behavior is of importance, perhaps he is wrong to display it.

When you couple this with rewarding acceptable behavior, you have a winning combination. When this winning combination is repeated, the message of it becomes instilled in a dog's mind; becoming part of his natural, automatic thinking process…And at that point you have success.

**The aspect of ignoring the puppy is crucial. Ignoring is not "mean"…It is actually a kind, gentle and non-reprimanding method to lead by example and show your puppy that all is fine. It will be by these actions (*or lack of them, actually*) that your puppy will be *reassured*. Soothing words and attention only serve to reinforce a puppy's perceived fear or intolerance.**

All dogs think of their human families as their "packs". Their human is the leader of the pack, known as the "Alpha". When a puppy shows negative behavior, if his leader shows that the behavior is not warranted, the puppy *will* take note of this message. It will mean a lot to him and when done enough, he will re-think his actions.

If a puppy barks at guests, if the leader's training for this involves ignoring the puppy, the puppy will learn that his barking behavior is *so* unwarranted that his leader is *oblivious* to it. If a puppy is afraid, shy or nervous and his leader ignores that behavior, the puppy will learn that since *his leader* is relaxed and confident, offering *no* soothing words, that being afraid, nervous or shy is *not* the correct response.

Therefore, you will speak with your guest and go about your business with them while *completely and utterly* ignoring whichever negative behavior your puppy is displaying. If he is hiding, do not try to encourage him to come out. If he is nudging at you, put on your best acting hat and behave as if you notice nothing at all. If he is barking, stay calm and pretend that you do not hear one "yap". If he is jumping up and down, imagine that he is invisible.

The *only* time that you should step in is if your puppy is *literally* jumping on your guest, causing them discomfort or injury. *If your guest can put up with some jumping that can be ignored, have them ignore it.* Everyone involved must ignore the puppy during this short time.

*Only* if this intense type of jumping is occurring should you then command your puppy into a "Down". You will wait 2-3 minutes before releasing him from the "Down". If he jumps on your guest again, bring him back to the "Down". If the puppy calms down and refrains from jumping, you will go back to completely ignoring him and then working forward as explained ahead.

## If your Puppy is Not Yet Trained for the "Down" Command

We will take a brief pause, in case your puppy is not yet trained to go "Down" upon command. *If your puppy is trained for this, feel free to move ahead.*

If not, and *if* your puppy is prone to jump up onto guests to a high enough level to cause discomfort that will need to be addressed and not ignored…Here is the training for this command:

The goal of this command will be that when the command "Down" is given, your dog will quickly lie down fully, without his rump sticking up; his belly will be flush down onto the floor. He will stay in this position until you give the release word.

Training sessions should last ten to fifteen minutes, done twice per day until the command is mastered. The command should be given at least one time per day afterward to reinforce the learned behavior.

Treats play a large role in enticing your puppy to follow this command. Therefore, your dog should be hungry when you do these training sessions. However, be sure that your dog is not starving for dinner as he will be too focused on wanting to devour a full meal to pay attention to you. He should be hungry enough that the treats are desired.

While each puppy learns at his own rate, if the training is done as often as described and it is done exactly as detailed ahead, your puppy may be able to master this command in one to three weeks.

End each session on a "high note" when your puppy is doing well, even if this means going back to a lower level of the training...so that you can end things by offering praise. Your puppy will be more prone to wanting to train for this the following days.

Give praise for "good attempts" and work to keep the moral high. Finally, never say "No" to correct him, say "Uh-oh" instead.

## Step-by-Step Instructions

❶ Choose a room that has little distractions. You may also wish to do this outside, but again it should be an area with few (or no) distractions.

❷ Have a treat in your hand, and also some in your pocket.

❸ Have your puppy on leash.

❹ With him facing you, hold a treat to his nose and lower it slowly to the floor. As you do this, say "Down" in a firm voice.

❺ In the best case scenario, your dog will simply follow the treat with his nose and lie down. If so, immediately give him the treat and praise him by saying, *"Good Down!"* Only release the treat while your dog is in the correct position. Do not give it to him if he gets up – that will be too late and he will think that you are rewarding the action of rising up.

If your puppy hunches over, slide the treat slowly toward him on the floor between his front paws or away from him. It may take a little time but he will ultimately lie down.

Remember to offer praise for good attempts as learning this may be done in increments. However, do not give the treat until he has mastered a full "Down".

❻ Once your puppy has shown you that he goes down when commanded in this way, move on to the stage of waiting a few seconds before giving him the reward. Remember to only reward while your dog is in the correct position of being flat on the floor. With your dog in a "Down", say, *"Wait...wait"* and then *"Good Down!"* while offering the treat.

❼ After your dog has the treat, release him from the "Down" by saying "Okay!" Say it as if you are saying, "You are free!" and use a hand motion to send that message. When your dog comes out of the down position, offer him praise and a pat. Do not offer a treat, but do make it clear that you are happy that he not only went down, but that he came out of the down when you released him with the release word of "Okay".

❽ Once your dog has mastered this, go up to the next stage of ordering "Down" in different situations. Ultimately you will want your dog to learn to drop "Down" when outside playing, when walking, when other people are around, etc. if you command for it.

*If your dog goes down, but then keeps getting up before you release him with the "Okay" release word:*

**1.** Do not offer the treat if he rises up before you say "Okay". Make sure that he sees the treat and try again.

**2.** There will be a first time that your dog does lie down and when you immediately give him the treat, and he will make the connection that a treat is only his when he goes down. Also, re-think your treat, it may need to be more special and surely a treat not ever given for a normal, regular snack.

**3.** Finally, for stubborn dogs, you can place your foot on the leash once the dog is down, which prevents him from being able to fully rise up.

**Tip**

Some owners use "Down" when they really want the dog to follow an "Off" command. "Off" will be used if your dog is sitting atop a chair that you placed your favorite shirt on or another scenario in which you really mean to say, "Please move!"

## Back to the Training

Unless you *absolutely* had to order your dog into a "Down" in order to stop any injury or discomfort to your guest, it will be important to not look at your puppy at all; and most importantly not to make eye contact. Do not use his name in the conversation that you are having with your guest.

At some point, out of a combination of exerting worthless energy and realizing that the negative behavior is getting him nowhere, he will pause. It is at the *very* moment of pausing, that you must take action.

Do be sure that the pause is not just done to take a breath. Wait for a count of 5 seconds. If he has stayed calm for full 5 seconds, immediately give praise. Remember that your tone of voice carries great meaning. Simply saying "Good Dog" with no enthusiasm is not going to mean a lot. When said with a happy, proud tone, it carries much more weight.

Give him a quick, loving pat and go back to speaking with your guest. You have now implanted the thought in your puppy's mind that when he stopped a behavior, he received attention (after being *clearly* ignored) in the form of praise and a pat.

If he reverts back to negative behavior, repeat the process of ignoring and only giving attention when there is a break of a solid and full 5 seconds.

If your puppy remains behaving nicely for the next 5 *minutes*, it is now time to further instill in his mind that his good behavior is not only noticed, but rewarded. It is time to give praise as described above, and offer the special treat that you have close at hand. Finish by getting down on your knee, close to your puppy and giving him a loving rub while talking in a calm yet happy voice.

Now, your puppy has learned that behaving nicely for a relatively good amount of time, thus proving himself and showing control equals a treat, praise and extra attention.

As the last step, you will go on to visit with your guest. If your puppy reverts to the negative behavior, you will go back to the step of ignoring and begin again. Remember, that if you give up on your puppy, he will never learn to behave appropriately. However, if you invest just a bit of time with this socialization training, you will forever have a well behaved dog.

If your puppy remains behaving as desired, you will have *your guest* offer a treat to him. Since you have gone through a process of teaching your puppy control and he is now calm, this training will finish off by teaching him that the guest is not a "foe" as your puppy once wondered about, but is a friend who can *also* produce benefits for your puppy.

*If the issue is that your puppy is shy,* he will ultimately venture out to say "Hello" or simply to find out why you are ignoring him. At that time you may feel so happy that you want to shower him with attention, kisses and praise. Your guest may also feel very enthusiastic…However, it is best to not overwhelm a shy puppy that found the bravery to interact a bit.

For this shy, nervous pup, speak to him in a matter-of-fact voice to show that you approve of his courage. Say, "Good Girl" or "Good Boy" in a happy, even manner while petting him just a bit. Then, go back to your conversation with your guest.

When you do this training for a shy or nervous puppy, there *will* be a point when he finds the courage to change his behavior. When he sees that by doing so, *nothing* bad happens and he is *actually* given praise, most often he will not revert back to hiding or feeling afraid.

If your puppy does not go back into hiding after 3 to 4 minutes, offer a treat. When your puppy reaches a point of showing relaxed interest in your guest, it is then that your guest should also offer a treat.

When training to reverse *any* negative behavior shown toward guests, whether you have just started training and your puppy has not yet stopped his negative behavior *or* if he has shown progress, the visit should only last for a maximum of 15 minutes.
It *can* be a longer visit the next time. If your puppy needs more training to find some success, it is best to not overwhelm him with this.

Even if he has shown progress, you will want to conclude the visit when you are able to end things on a good note. If a visit is allowed to be an extended one, your puppy may end up losing control and/or tolerance and it can negate all that was learned.

When this is done just one time, it is a temporary lesson. If this is done once when a guest comes over, but then is not done the next time a visitor comes by…and the training is not consistent, it will not bring about fully learned lessons, and it will only serve to confuse your puppy.

When it is done consistently, each and every time that a guest comes over and if you have the patience to follow through with each step until things end on a good note, your puppy will be successful in regard to his socialization skills with that guest.

The majority of puppies will learn that this lesson applies to all guests that you welcome into the home. In rare cases, a puppy will associate this lesson to that *one* certain person. It is uncommon, but if that is the case, he or she will need to be trained for each person who regularly comes over to your home.

# Strangers, Dogs and Other Triggers – Teaching Your Puppy to be Well Behaved No Matter Where You Go

A puppy cannot be expected to behave in a well-mannered way or to embrace every situation with a cheerful attitude when those things are new to him…Or if he has been forced to experience them for an extended amount of time without having gradual, incremental exposure.

It is best to have involvement in a new activity, exposure to a new environment, or interaction in a new situation be a gradual, incremental experience *even before* you learn if it is going to be a problem for your puppy. If you do this, it most likely will never become a problem at all. If you wait and find out that it is a problem, you will then need to invest time to reverse the behavior.

Therefore, while the list can be seemingly endless, here are the most common things that your puppy should be slowly exposed to (and we will go into detail ahead):

*Encountering Strangers* – This can occur in the pet supply store, while taking your daily walk or while out in public in any location.

*Other Dogs* – Typically, encounters will occur at the dog park or the pet supply store. Your puppy may also need to become used to your neighbor's dog(s).

*Traffic* – Most often encountered while taking a walk with you on the side of a busy street, but some dogs are also afraid or wary of traffic that passes by the home.

*Other Pets* - If you had a current pet when you brought your puppy into your home, chances are that they learned to know each other and are getting along fine. If not, we will discuss this ahead. Most of the time socialization to other pets will need to be done if a new pet is about to be introduced into your household in which your dog is already an established member.

*Riding in your Car* – Some dogs hardly notice that a car is moving; others not only notice that it is moving, but can be terribly afraid of it and/or develop motion sickness.

# The Process for Meet and Greets with Strangers

For encountering strangers, this will be a matter of showing your puppy how to interact (or avoid) and to correct any actions that are not a part of a well socialized display of behavior.

When out in public and encountering strangers, this is one of the most typical times that an owner can feel the heavy weight of trying to deal with a puppy that is not socialized. And for a puppy, without lessons learned, this can be a very overwhelming situation.

As you work on this, things will gradually become better for both of you. You will not dread excursions and the chaos that may accompany them as much...And your puppy will look forward to venturing out, as he gains self-confidence and self-control.

If the route that you take for your daily walk does not often bring you by other people (or does not present an opportunity to engage with others), it is best to choose one place to visit, one time per week that will allow you to socialize your puppy to strangers.

The dog park will certainly be such a place, however if you still need to teach your puppy how to behave with other dogs, this may be too much since he will need to deal with two new elements: strangers *and* unknown dogs.

Better would be an outdoor mall, a neighborhood yard sale, a small flea market, an outdoor patio of a coffee shop that permits dogs in their outside seating area, a local baseball game, a hiking trail, the outdoor seating area of a local ice cream shop (weather permitting), or a smaller park that is not an official "dog park" but does allow dogs...There are many such parks that simply require that the dog be leashed.

You will need 3 things to be in order before beginning: Having your puppy on harness, having treats on you and making sure that your puppy follows the "Sit" command.

 *It is recommended, as discussed earlier, to have your puppy on harness as opposed to collar.* This is best for all toy and small dog breeds at all times, and works well for medium, large and giant breeds as a method to have better control.

 ***Be sure to have some treats on you,*** preferably in your pocket book or pockets, hidden from your puppy, for reward during socialization to people.

 ***In regard to the "Sit" command,*** when you are ready for your puppy to interact with a stranger, you will command him to sit.

You *may* have seen references elsewhere that claim that an owner should ask the stranger to command the puppy to sit. **This is not a good idea!**

It is a ***terrible*** idea to have *anyone* other than the puppy's direct human leaders to command him. Giving commands shows leadership. A puppy learns to follow the commands of their "pack leaders". This is a part of establishing your authority, and in turn, good behavior. If complete strangers, and a lot of them, are giving commands to your puppy, this rescinds all that you were working for to have your puppy see you as his leader.

If your puppy does not know the "Sit" command yet or is still in the process of learning we will now look at one of the most effective and fastest methods to reach success quickly. When followed, a puppy can learn the "Sit" command in one to three weeks. It will be important to offer short 10 minute lessons, a minimum of 2 times per day and up to 3 to 4 times per day if you have the time.

### Teaching the "Sit" Command

The goal of this command will be that when the command "Sit" is given, your dog will sit squarely and firmly down on his hindquarters and remain sitting until you give the "release" word.

Puppies as young as seven weeks old can start learning this command and it is often the first command that a dog is taught. This command is the foundation for essentially all other commands. Have at least two training sessions each day. It is best to have them be spaced apart, with perhaps one in the morning and one in the early evening. If morning is not a good time for you, you can practice once in the early evening and once a couple of hours later but not within an hour of "bedtime".

Treats play a huge role in enticing your puppy to follow this command. Therefore, your dog should be hungry when you do these training sessions. However, be sure that your dog is not starving for dinner as he will be too focused on wanting to devour a full meal and not be able to stay focused. He should be hungry enough that the treats are desired.

End on a "high note" when your puppy is doing well. Give praise for "good attempts" and work to keep the morale high. Finally, never say "No" and to say "Uh-oh" instead.

### Step-by-Step Instructions

❶ Choose a room that has little distractions. You may also wish to do this outside, but again it should be an area with few (or no) distractions.

❷ Have a treat in your hand, and also some in your pocket.

❸ Have your puppy on leash.

❹ Stand or kneel right in front of him, holding a treat in your hand a little higher than your dog's head.

❺ Slowly move the treat *straight back over* his head. This should cause his nose to point up and his rump to drop down to the floor. If his rump does not drop, keep moving the treat straight backward toward his tail. The very moment that his rump touches the floor, give him the treat and signal the desired behavior by saying, "Good Sit!" in a happy voice.

**Note:** It is important to say "Good SIT" and not "Good Boy" or "Good Girl" because saying "Good *Sit!*" reinforces the command, allowing your dog to have a better understanding of why he is being rewarded.

❻ Once your dog has shown you that he sits when commanded in this way, move on to the stage of waiting a few seconds before giving him the reward. Remember to only reward while your dog is in the correct position of squarely sitting on the floor.

Slowly increase the amount of time that you wish for your dog to sit. Start with just a count of three seconds. During the time that you want your puppy to say in a "Sit" position, say "Wait...*Wait*..."

❼ When you are ready for him to come out of the "Sit", say "Okay" (the release word). Say it as if you are saying, "You are free!" and use a hand motion to send that message. When your dog moves out of the sitting position, offer him praise and a pat. Do not offer a treat, but do make it clear that you are happy that he not only sat, but came out of the sit when you released him with the word of "Okay".

### Back to the Process with Strangers

When you are out and about with your puppy, the first step is to simply walk among other people. Your dog should be to your left. This is the standard positioning for proper heeling; and it is good for your puppy to always understand that your left side is his "starting" and "ending" point.

When out in public and later on when you are exploring the world together, your puppy (soon to be your adult dog) will feel safer and you will have more control if he is to your left as opposed to anywhere that he wishes.

Whether you have a retractable leash or a standard six foot leash, you will want to adjust the length so that your puppy cannot go out further than a foot from you. In this manner, walk among other people and talk to your puppy while doing so. Let him take in the new sounds, smells and become familiar with the activity that occurs in groups of people.

Undoubtedly there will be people who come up to you to comment on your puppy and ask to pet him. This is your opportunity for one-on-one socialization.

## Making a Decision about a Meet and Greet

It is at this point that you will decide if your puppy is ready for one-one-one physical interaction which we will refer to as a Meet and Greet. Not all puppies will be ready on Day One. For some, just being in a crowd of people is enough for the day. For those puppies, just enjoy strolling around people and be proud that your puppy is taking this first step. You can most likely move on to the second step the next time or on the third time.

The way that you will know if your puppy is ready for a Meet and Greet with a stranger is by how your puppy behaves when a stranger approaches. If your puppy is anxious and you force him to interact, it will do more harm than good. Forcing interaction can cause a puppy to become more fearful...And when a dog displays clear signals that he does not want interaction with a stranger, trying to *make* it happen can even lead to a biting incident.

Remember, socialization is a gradual process.

If your puppy shows: excessive lip licking, keeps turning his head side to side, tries to back away and/or growls, he is not yet ready. The stronger the signs, the more time you need to spend just walking in crowds until he is so accustomed to it (and has learned that nothing bad comes of it) that he will *then* be ready to Meet and Greet.

## Continuing on with the Meet and Greet

If your puppy is calm when someone approaches to comment on him or asks to pet him, do explain to that person that you are in the process of training your puppy to be socialized and then ask that person to please give your puppy a small treat (that you hand over to the person) *if* your puppy behaves for them. Most people will be more than happy to assist.

Command your puppy to sit. Ask the person to please pet him from the same level as your dog. This will mean, depending on the size of your puppy, that the person bends over slightly or kneels down. If all strangers interact with your puppy from a standing position it will cause too much of an intimidation factor.

Additionally, while your puppy may have not minded being picked up by strangers when younger, as we discussed earlier, as he grows and is more aware of the world, the puppy will be choosier about who picks him up. Your puppy needs to trust you that when you both go out in public that it does not equal you allowing strangers to keep handling him.

Once your puppy sits, be sure to offer praise of "Good Sit" (Reinforcing the "sit" command as discussed earlier) and "Good Dog" to show praise for staying in the sit position.

Allow that person to pet your dog. You *may* need to encourage your puppy to remain sitting by saying "Wait...*Wait*..." as you did while training him to sit. With some puppies, an owner will not need to offer any words.

While a person may want to pet your puppy for quite a while (children could sit there for an hour to pet and play), it is best to keep meetings short until your puppy is used to interacting with all sorts of people. You will then have a better understanding of his tolerance level and his level of interest to either be petted or to play with children.

Therefore, while you do not need to officially time it, a Meet and Greet of 30 seconds to 1 minute is best. You can explain to the person that you are keeping initial meetings short for now. Ask that person to end things on a good note and have them offer the small treat (that you had given to them earlier) to your puppy.

With the treat being small (just a tad of a taste to show a job well done) within a second or so, you can give the release word of "Okay" and move on to walking among "strangers".

## Troubleshooting the Process for Greeting Strangers

If your puppy jumps up on a person: Keep the leash short, so that this is not physically possible at first. This is why a harness is strongly recommended; with a dog collar, jumping can cause injury to a dog's neck. Let the person know that part of the training is for jumping and to please turn to the side if the puppy jumps so that the puppy's attempts are in vain and then to ignore the puppy.

Even if your puppy only jumps on people randomly, still follow all of the training instructions so that your puppy learns that jumping equals a turned shoulder and zero attention *and* that *not* jumping equals a friendly pet and a treat as discussed previously.

## Moving Ahead

Always end things on a good note; your excursion to the outdoor mall or any other place that you have chosen should come to a finish while your puppy is behaving very well. For a puppy that is new to all of this, 30 minutes to one hour is the maximum time that one should expect him to have tolerance for this, as things may seem overwhelming if in a crowd much longer than that on Day One.

Increase Meet and Greets as your puppy learns to handle them. Normally within 8-10 outings, most puppies will become familiarized enough with this aspect of the world that they will be ready to handle strangers in just about any situation.

Once this aspect of meeting strangers is complete, you can move on to meeting dogs, which will then involve a Meet and Greet with both dogs *and* their owners (and your puppy will already be used to one of those elements). This introduction to other dogs will be discussed in the following chapter.

# The Process for Meet and Greets with Other Dogs

While most dogs do not *need* to be "friends" with other canines, it is best to socialize your puppy to other dogs. Why? There are many answers!

 It greatly decreases the chances that your puppy (and then older dog) will have a lifetime of barking or disturbance behavior upon hearing, seeing or picking up the scent of another dog.

 It cuts down on the chances of your puppy growing up to show aggression toward other dogs.

 If you ever bring another dog into the home, it will make for a much easier transition.

 If you live in a neighborhood with other pet owners, it allows your puppy to learn to be a "good neighbor", which often counts for a lot in a neighborhood of adjacent homes in which you may wish to help contribute toward creating an atmosphere of friendliness and sociability.

You will want your puppy (and soon to be adult dog)

to be prepared for many things; and meeting other dogs is a fact of life. You will want him to have the confidence to perform the Meet and Greet in the way that canines are meant to and have been doing for thousands of years. Trying to inhibited and repress this instinct is not beneficial.

## The "Canine Hello"

Before you take your puppy to commence Meet and Greets with other dogs, let's go over what to expect. One of the most common things that will happen is that the dogs will sniff each other. While some will sniff the other's face or entire body, most will sniff near the genitals of the other dog.

Dogs sniff each other in this way for a very precise reason and while a human may think that it is unnecessary (and possibly unsanitary), an owner should never try to force a dog to suppress this instinct. Sniffing near each other's genitals is not just an arbitrary area that dogs "somehow" got into a habit of doing.

While it may appear that the dogs are sniffing at the genitals, they are actually sniffing the anal area – this is done for a very valid canine reason, as discussed ahead.

Dogs interpret others using sight, sound and smell. While humans generally rely mostly on their sight for input regarding another person, a dog will heavily rely on their sense of smell. For a canine, the sense of smell is used as the main method of interpretation an average 55% of the time, much more than humans use it.

You may already be aware that your puppy has anal glands as it is an element of grooming. They are small, often the size of a pea. There are two, with each being located on opposite sides of the rectum opening.

Each dog has a distinct and individual smell that emits from these glands. A canine, by sniffing this odor of another dog, will be able to learn vital information about him. Since dogs cannot ask each other about themselves, this way of "finding out" about another dog is important.

The scent emitted tells a dog: The gender of the other, the health status of the other and the temperament of the other. Therefore, your puppy, when sniffing another dog, will know within seconds if the dog is female or male….If the dog has any health issues….and if the dog is friendly or is a potential foe.

When both dogs have assimilated the information received and both are satisfied that a meeting would be beneficial, the dogs will continue on to Meet and Greet.

## First, Meet the Neighbor Dogs and Friends' Dogs

Beginning this training with somewhat "known" dogs is best as you will have more control to help your puppy learn this before attempting socialization with unknown dogs encountered at the park, etc.

Keeping in mind the way that dogs instinctually and naturally greet each other, an owner does not need to do much, other than to *initiate* the Meet and *supervise* the Greet.

With friends or family, arranging a time for this is all that is needed to begin. For neighboring dogs, it is best to plan for this as opposed to having your puppy encounter them while out for a walk.

Therefore if you are friendly with any neighbors who are dog owners, you can agree to meet and allow the dogs to get to know each other.

If you do not know a neighbor very well, this is a good opportunity to get to know them. If this is what you wish to do, it is suggested to say hello and introduce yourself without having your puppy with you. Once doing so, you can let them know that you have a new puppy (or dog) and so that everyone gets along well you wish to bring him over for a Meet and Greet at a convenient time.

Elsewise you can wait until encounters occur while out walking in the neighborhood; however when you plan this out you can be better prepared.

 **When doing a Meet and Greet with known dogs, if you have an unneutered male and he will be meeting a female, check in advance to make sure that the female is not in**

**heat. If you have an un-spayed female, and she will be meeting an unneutered male, never allow this to occur if she is in heat.**

**If you have an un-spayed female, when she is in heat it is suggested to limit walks or outings to any place in which there may be male dogs. The mating urge that un-neutered male dogs have can be extremely strong...A male can injure a female if trying to force a "mount"...And of course, you will not want to allow a situation that can result in an unplanned breeding and resulting litter.**

You will never want to drop your puppy from the leash. As talked about earlier, it is highly suggested to have a harness on your puppy as opposed to a collar. This can be especially helpful when encountering another dog. If there is opposition and any jumping occurs, you can safely bring your puppy back to you without putting any undue pressure on the neck.

It is best to talk to your puppy in a relaxed, calm voice as the dogs first take note of each other. After that, your puppy probably will not be focusing on your voice very much, if at all. Therefore, take that short window of opportunity to relay that you are calm and relaxed, as your puppy will often read your tone of voice and pick up on the vibes that you are sending.

Keeping the leash out long enough to allow freedom of movement, permit your puppy and the other dog to sniff each other as described earlier. They will then decide if they wish to continue on to play, etc.

If the other dog backs off and does not show interest in playing, do not take it personally. There are many reasons why another dog may do this. If he or she is an older dog, they merely may not have the personality that wants to romp around with a puppy. No matter what their ages, the dogs may find out during the exchange of information that they are not well-suited playmates. It is best to just be happy that your puppy was successful with the "Meet" portion.

If the two dogs appear to be getting along, they may wish to play and this will often occur if both dogs are puppies. This is fine as long as both are on leash. Only *after* one successful "Greet" is it then suggested to allow two certain puppies to play off leash in a safely enclosed yard.

Similar to when your puppy needed to learn that you were the "leader" and the "Alpha" of the pack (your family), the 2 dogs often will play a "game" to establish who the "Alpha" is out of the two of *them*. When dogs are near each other, one will claim the "Alpha" position and the other(s) will accept Beta position(s). This is normal.

The dog that is not Alpha should not be considered the "loser". It is pure canine instinct for one dog to be dominant over the other. Usually, it will be the male if one dog is male and one is female. With same gender dogs, if one is older than the other, then the older one will often seek the Alpha position.

The decision about "Who is Alpha?" will often occur without you even knowing. However, if both dogs wish to be the governing one and if each firmly "demands" to be the "Alpha", they may begin to fight.

This is most often preceded by warnings. The warnings can include growls, baring teeth, standing off to face each other, tensing into a fighting stance and/or direct staring into each other's eyes. If any of this occurs, immediately separate the two dogs (this is why when first meeting, they must stay on leash even when in an enclosed yard).

With two puppies, if they wish to establish which one will be the "leader", it most often happens during play and more specifically, while wrestling.

Owners must learn to recognize what is play and what is not. Any warning signs as mentioned earlier are signs of actual aggression and the dogs should immediately be separated. If, while playing, one dog nips (NOT bites) the other, the "victim" may let out a "yelp" and ignore the offender for a brief time...If the other dog's body language demonstrates remorse, he will often go back to playing with the understanding that nipping done too roughly will not be tolerated.

 **Note: A nip is a quick snapping of the jaws that may or may not make contact (some nips are into the air). It does not break skin or cause anything other than a fast, slight discomfort. A *bite* is an aggressive sinking of the teeth into the skin, blood is drawn...This is violent, intolerable behavior – the dogs must be separated and the injury must be treated. This will be rare as most canines will display the warnings signs discussed earlier...The dogs will be separated, preventing a bite.**

If both puppies appear to be tolerating each other but are not playing on their own, you can enter the picture and encourage play. Tossing a ball to them works well and if one certain dog is clearly the faster runner, tossing two balls (one to each dog) should keep both happy.

End the meeting on a good note, when your puppy is behaving. You can offer treats to both dogs (with the permission of the other dog's owner of course) to show that you are proud that your puppy handled things well. When done in this way, your puppy or dog will be less likely to bark at either your neighbor or his dog. Therefore, this is a socialization lesson well worth teaching.

For neighbors that you know well and consider to be friends, you may wish to set up weekly or monthly "play dates", but do be aware that dogs do not "need" friends as most humans do. Being with you and your immediate family, staying active with walks and exercise, enjoying play time with you, being brought along for events like running at the beach or going for a hike and appreciating the moments of resting beside you at home on the sofa is enough to keep a dog happy and fulfilled.

While play dates with other dogs that your puppy gets along with is not a bad thing and your dog may enjoy that time, play dates are not "needed" to occur to create a balanced life. This is overstated because some busy owners feel overwhelmed and put pressure on themselves to continually set up play dates for their dog when it crams too much into an already busy day. Teaching your puppy socialization is the focus, so that he will be prepared for any meetings, whether planned or not planned.

# Encountering Unknown "Stranger" Dogs

At various times your puppy will encounter dogs that are "strangers". This is inevitable since you will be taking your puppy for daily walks and trying to expand his world by bringing him to dog parks and to other locations.

Not every dog is going to be a friend. There will always more aggressive dogs that warrant both you and your puppy staying away.

Whenever you head out with your puppy to go somewhere, always bring treats with you. You *will* want to be able to reward a job well done if an opportunity arises to meet "stranger" dogs, but *also* for many other good shows of behavior that your puppy may display.

If another dog is *not* showing signs of aggression (staring intently, baring teeth, growling, taking a firm stance, etc.), then do allow your puppy to follow canine instinct and allow the dogs to sniff each other as discussed earlier.

Whenever your dog behaves well around another dog, after approximately 5 minutes, end the session (so that you end on a high note) and give praise and then reward. After your puppy has built up enough skills to do well with other dogs on a consistent basis, time spent playing and interacting can increase if you wish.

If your dog is not behaving nicely, firmly lead him away and allow him a rest before meeting any other dogs. It may just be a matter of needing to "regroup", especially if your puppy has already said "hello" to several dogs during the excursion; he may be feeling a little overwhelmed.

While you are taking a rest, keep him beside you on leash. Do not give a treat when the rest is over. Simply allow him an opportunity to enter the situation again and demonstrate better behavior.
Any time that he *does* prove better behavior than before, offer praise and a treat.

If encounters do not go well at all, this means that your puppy needs shorter sessions. Some owners reverse course and *back away* from Meet and Greets….They believe that since their dog did not do well, that it is best to stop putting their dog into a Meet and Greet situation. *But this is not the answer.* Avoidance of a trigger of negative behavior will *never* be beneficial. A puppy will need *more* exposure, not less. That exposure should, however, be at shorter intervals, allowing a puppy to have a more gradual experience.

As time goes by, your puppy *will* gain self-confidence when encountering other dogs. You will have allowed him to know that he has the freedom to sniff other dogs to learn about them. You will keep him in control with harness and leash but will have also taught him that you allow freedom for the "Greeting" portion, should it take place and that you also allow freedom for play, should it take place.

You will have taught your puppy that dogs come in all sizes, ages and have various temperaments. Your puppy will learn that some dogs are friends, some are foes and some will be "neutral" animals that warrant a "Meet" but you are not forcing a "Greet".

By exposing your puppy to all sorts of dogs, he will have a good understanding of the various scenarios that can play out. You will have taught him that behaving nicely brings about good things (praise and reward) and any negative behavior will begin to cease as a canine always learns to choose which action brings about the most benefits.

# Helping Your Dog Tolerate Traffic

One element that can be frustrating for owners is when their puppy shows signs of either being disturbed by traffic (barking) or of being afraid of traffic (cowering, reluctance to walk on the sidewalk). This can cause walks to be troublesome; you expected to enjoy your daily walks with your puppy and now you may dread them.

If a puppy is exposed to the sights, sounds and smells of traffic at an early age, all of this can be avoided. If your puppy has suddenly shown signs of distress when near traffic, this can be fixed.

In both cases, the goal will be to introduce the element of traffic in a gradual way, and as your dog learns to handle one level, you will then take things up a notch. As he gains self-confidence with a small amount of traffic, it will prepare him to deal with increasing, more intense situations. When done properly, a dog can have tolerance when walking alongside the busiest of streets.

Therefore, whether you are just starting to socialize your puppy to this element or you are planning on retraining your dog for this, it will all begin in the same way as described ahead.

## Introduction to Traffic

It is best to train your puppy to tolerate traffic *before* he gains any fear of it. This section will cover the details of how to introduce your puppy to traffic if it is new to him and you are just *now* ready to start taking daily walks.

We will go over the basics, and then based on how your puppy behaves, dive deeper into training for specific behaviors.

If you live on a very busy street, to begin to socialize your puppy to traffic, you will need to find a quiet area for your walks. Socialization requires an introduction to an element and then a gradual increase to  that element. Therefore, if you live on a street that has cars always zooming by, your puppy cannot learn tolerance if you begin at such an intense level.

Best is to find a quiet neighborhood with barely a car driving by. Your goal will be to choose a location that *does* have cars, but *not* a *steady* flow of traffic. While you certainly cannot control the flow of automobiles, best would be an area in which 2 to 3 cars pass by within a time window of 20 to 30 minutes.

To prepare to head out, have your puppy on harness (as described earlier to both prevent injury and to have better control). You will also want to bring along treats in order to immediately reward good behavior.

With your puppy on your left, begin your walk. When you notice that a car is heading your way and is going to pass you, begin speaking to your puppy in a casual, relaxed tone. This is done to both distract your puppy and to set up the ambiance of a calm atmosphere.

Be sure that you continue walking; however do try to keep your puppy's attention on you. If it appears that your puppy did not even notice the car at all, as they were seemingly focused on something else (bugs, grasses, the sound of birds, etc. or your voice as you are speaking matter-of-factly) do know that your puppy was indeed also aware of the car.

With incredible canine senses, if he did not look at the car, he most certainly sensed it with both smell and hearing.

In this case, once the car has passed, immediately offer praise of "Good Boy", or "Good Girl" and then give reward. Once done, do not stay still but simply continue on with the walk.

If your puppy *looks* at the car but withholds from barking, trying to run away or cowering in fear, also give praise and reward as described.

If your puppy is doing well, repeat a walk in this area each day for one week. Then during the second week, choose an area that offers more traffic, but again, not a steady flow. If all goes well, on the third week you can bring your puppy on street of varying intensities of traffic as he has proven that he has successfully built up a suitable tolerance.

*Only* move up to a new level of intensity once your puppy has mastered the current level. Moving up before your puppy is ready will only backfire.

Remember to always stay on the sidewalk. It is a shame when owners are seen walking their dogs right alongside traffic when the sidewalk is either right beside them or simply on the opposite side of the street. Crossing the road is highly preferable to walking any amount of distance with cars zooming alongside only feet (if not inches) away.

## Troubleshooting - If Your Dog Barks at Traffic

If your puppy or dog has proven that his response to cars is *excessive* barking, distraction training will need to be done during socialization training.

You will prepare for a walk in the same way as described earlier, by choosing a route with a small amount of traffic and by having treats on you to give as reward. New to this will be a distraction element. While you can be creative and use a variety of different methods, great success can been found with a simple metal container filled with pennies.

Best is a metal container that is small enough to fit in your pocket or in your hand. Action must be done quickly and you will not have time to go searching for it in a bag or backpack. Pennies (or any other object that will make a rattling noise) should be placed inside; but not too many that they do not have room to move. The goal is to create a "noisemaker".

Walk with confidence and be sure that your voice does not send a message of apprehension that a car *will* pass by.

When a car is approaching, get ready. As the car reaches a distance that your puppy would normally bark, quickly and assertively toss the noisemaker on the ground in the *opposite* direction of the car, which will cause your puppy to turn around to see what made the noise. While your puppy is looking away in reaction to the noise, the car will pass by.

Once this has happened, say "Good Boy" or "Good Girl", offer a pat and a treat. Casually pick up the noisemaker and continue on.

If your puppy was not distracted by the noisemaker, the noisemaker was not loud enough. You will either need to add more pennies, choose a different container, toss it with more force or toss it a closer distance from your puppy (but of course not close enough to scare him… as only "distraction" is the goal).

When you learn which created noisemaker (thrown at the right force and distance and at the right timing) causes your puppy to turn and notice *it* instead of noticing and barking at the *car*, you have found success and are on your way to final victory.

Your puppy has now learned that the car was not as important as another source of noise/movement. Your puppy has now learned that when his attention was placed elsewhere and he did not bark at the car, it was beneficial to him in the form of praise and a treat.

Do remember that one outing such as this does not equal a dog that is socialized to traffic. Lessons must be instilled. Therefore, this should be repeated for at least one week before you move things up a level to walking on a street with a higher degree of traffic. Only move up to a higher level of intensity (more traffic) if your puppy has mastered the current level.

## Troubleshooting - If Your Dog is Afraid of Traffic

Another common reaction that a puppy or dog can have to traffic is that of being fearful. This is understandable since canines have no real sense of what automobiles are. To them, they are large and loud objects moving closer and closer. A fearful dog does not yet have 100% assurance that a car will not physically touch him. Even if he has seen 100 cars pass by, he may still not feel safe that cars do not present a danger. For a dog that is fearful, he will be afraid of *potential* danger.

While it is done with good intentions, one of the biggest mistakes that owners make is to soothe or comfort their dog when the dog is afraid. They feel that if they offer comfort, it will teach their dog that all is fine. This is not true. In most cases, doing this will actually teach a dog that he is "correct" to be afraid.

It is human instinct to offer comfort when someone is afraid or upset; wanting to do this for your puppy is no exception. However, in order to help your puppy learn that he need not be afraid of something, an owner must train in a way that makes sense to a canine and provide words and actions that translate the intended message as a canine will interpret it.

When an owner speaks in a soft, comforting voice and says things such as "It's okay", "Don't be afraid", "It will be alright", etc. this is the same as telling a dog, "You are correct in being afraid, oh yes, this is *very* frightening, hopefully it will be over soon, don't worry, I will protect you".

If an owner *picks up their puppy* and cuddles him in an attempt to soothe him, this sends out a strong signal that *not only* is something "truly scary" but that it is *also* terrifying enough that the puppy needs physical protection in the form of being lifted from the ground and held.

Therefore, by trying to comfort a dog, an owner can instill the notion that cars are terrifying, scary things.

When an owner has established themselves as the dog's leader, this does more than allow that owner to better train and shape the behavior of the dog. It also gives the dog reassurance to follow the lead of that person. Therefore, if an established leader is tense, the dog will become tense. If the leader is happy, the dog will act happy. If the leader is calm, the dog will be become calm.

Now that we know what words and actions, however well intended, will make things worse and we know why words and actions can mean so much to a dog, let's look at what is best to say and do.

Quite contrary to offering comfort, when a dog shows fear of traffic, the owner must show by example that there is nothing to be afraid of. You will always be there to protect your puppy....Therefore, do not feel that the following method is akin to "leaving your dog on their own"....It is not. What you will be doing is leading by example and giving your puppy an opportunity to gain self-confidence.

The best method for socializing a puppy or dog when they are fearful of traffic is to completely ignore any displays of fear. A puppy may try to cling to you, he may cower down, he may whine, he may turn and tuck his tail down and/or shake.

It will not matter what your puppy does...Your goal will be to walk with confidence despite any of this, which will ultimately transfer that confidence to your dog.

Your goal will be to begin on a street with very little traffic. This means that for a 15 to 20 minute walk, perhaps 1 to 2 cars pass by. Any more than this will be overwhelming if the dog is very fearful of automobiles. Obviously, you cannot control the movement of the traffic; so you will find that some days bring 1 passing car and another day may bring 3 or 4...And this is alright. Your job will be to find a location to walk that offers the best chances of 1 to 2 cars driving by, on average, during your walk.

Be prepared by having your puppy on harness (as talked about earlier for to prevent neck injury and for better control) and have treats with you for reward.

Have your puppy on your left side (as we discussed earlier as this is the side for proper heeling) and as you walk, talk! You will want to talk to your puppy in a relaxed and matter-of-fact way, keeping in mind that you do not want to sound comforting or soothing (as described earlier).

It does not matter what you talk about...you can tell you puppy about your day at work or you can recap your favorite television show...All that matters is that your puppy becomes aware that you are in a calm mood with no trepidation or fear.

When a car inevitably passes by, do not tense up in anticipation. Continue walking. Your puppy may attempt to plant himself down firmly or try to lie down. This is one reason the harness comes in handy.

Keeping the same steady pace, continue walking, as if you are completely and utterly unaware that your puppy is attempting to either stay still or drop down. With the harness displacing pressure across the back, shoulders and chest (and not the neck as a collar would) you will cause no harm to him as long as you do not run.... Just walk at the normal pace that you established as your walk began.

If your puppy whines, continue talking about the TV show or your work day or whatever subject you were speaking about. Your goal is to entirely act as if you do not notice any change in your puppy's behavior. You will want to continue on as if the car was no more important than a passing butterfly.

As the car drives by and is then gone from sight, your puppy is going to become confused for a moment.

The thoughts that will momentarily pass through his mind are metaphorically going to be: "Oh my Gosh, that was *terrifying*, why in the *world* did my owner *not* notice that horribly scary thing!", "I am *shocked* that my leader continued to walk as if that scary object did not exist... did my leader not notice that I was trying to blend in with the sidewalk?"....

"*Wait a moment*... things are *starting* to become a bit clearer...my leader, the person that I depend on for *survival*, was *not* afraid of that car at all, *in fact* he ignored it completely...*Could it be?*....*Perhaps* it is.... Yes, *perhaps* I was wrong to think that the car was scary"....

And now you are on your way to success. You have taught your puppy to rethink his reaction. You have taught your puppy to *consider* the fact that perhaps cars are not scary.

This is a turning point; *but* by no means will the training be done in one lesson.

Now that you have taught your puppy to rethink his reaction, it is only by repeating this lesson will you then allow your puppy to not only rethink his reaction, but to strongly consider reacting in the opposite way. By repeating *further*, you will *then* allow your puppy to not only *consider* reacting without fear, but to actually *do so*.

When you repeat this lesson enough that your puppy handles a passing car without showing signs of fear, it is now time to give praise and reward. Remember, earlier you were using *all* of your willpower to ignore him; therefore rewards did not come into play. Now, you are at the point that good behavior receives both praise and reward.

After one week of handling a certain intensity of traffic in a calm manner, you can then take things up one level, choosing a walking route that is a bit busier. Handle each passing car as described earlier...ignoring the negative behavior and marking good behavior with reward.

# Other Pets – Creating a Home of Peace, Happiness and Friendship

Other pets will come into play in one of two different ways: Either you will bring a new puppy into a household in which there are already other pets or you will decide to bring a new pet into the home that your puppy lives in.

In either case, the best process is to never make a commitment to bring one animal into the home as a pet until you have tested both animals to see if they will tolerate each other.

Owners must take into consideration the known temperament of the dog breed, both of the currently owned dog and the dog that one is considering bringing into the home. Some breeds simply do not tolerate other dogs or other animals.

The Akita, for example, is known to have little to no tolerance for other dogs, particularly those of the same gender. To bring an Akita into the home of another dog...Or to try to bring home a new puppy in an Akita household is simply asking for failure. Fighting will ensue and one or both dogs can receive severe injuries; and injuries can even be fatal.

Crossbred dogs can have the same temperament of either parent, therefore the crossed mix of two purebred dogs should be considered to have the same tolerance or intolerance traits of his parents, unless proven otherwise.

With hundreds of purebred dog breeds *and* crosses that exist (intentional breeding of two different purebreds resulting in a "hybrid" or "designer" dog) there is no reasonable method of listing out which types of dogs may or may not get along...as there are roughly 270,000 possible combinations. Therefore, an owner should learn about the expected temperaments of both animals before considering having a multi-dog household.

**In regard to pet ownership statistics, 28% of dog owners have 2 dogs and 12% of dog owners have 3 or more dogs.**

Concerning the tolerance of other animals such as cats, hamsters, ferrets and the like, breed temperament plays a huge role in expected tolerance. Some breeds have strong hunting instinct and will have urges to chase smaller creatures. It is hoped that an owner understands the nature of the breed of dog involved as to not ever create a situation that is bound to end badly.

## Testing for Possible Friendship

Whether your puppy would be coming into the home with a current pet or your potential new pet would be introduced into the home of your puppy, testing should be done first. The result will hopefully show 1 of 3 things: Possible friendship, potential foes or tolerance.

## Signs of Potential Trouble

With dogs or with a dog/cat combination, if the animals stare intently at each other, if there is growling (dogs) or hissing (cats), pacing and signs of nervousness, baring of teeth, hairs standing on end, and/or attempted biting or nipping this means that the two animals will have little to no tolerance for each other.

If one animal behaves fine, but the other shows signs of intolerance, this also will mean a high probability of potential trouble.

## Signs of Potential Friendship

If the two animals investigate each other and then show no signs of hostility, this is obviously a good sign. Additionally, if the two animals pay no attention to each other, this is usually also a good sign. While the two may never be best friends, disregarding each other is a sign that neither sees the other as a threat. In time, bonding may start and increase and the two may very well end up being best buddies.

If the above applies, it is suggested to have two "Meet and Greets" to be sure that there is a tolerance.

## Helping Your Puppy Be Comfortable with Another Pet

Nothing should be forced; two animals that tolerate each other should be allowed to proceed at whatever pace they feel comfortable with. If you have an older dog and a young puppy, you need to be aware that the older dog may have a low level of patience for the actions of a puppy, and with valid reason.

Puppies often are full of energy and are very active; older dogs have  reached a point in their lives where they feel very safe and secure in the family....wishing often to just rest and relax. If a puppy starts to crawl over him in an attempt to play, a much older and serious dog cannot be expected to be a playmate in return.

Here are some tips to keep in mind to create a happy household.

 Two puppies will often engage in play and that play may involve nipping. If a puppy nips and the other yelps out in reaction, if the offending puppy backs off and does not nip again, all will sort itself out. If the offending puppy continues to nip, he or she should be removed and isolated from the other.

The puppy being isolated should be allowed to see what he is missing out on, but completely ignored, by withholding both actions (touching or picking up the puppy) and words. After a 5 to 10 minute "time out", he can be let back in to play, but must be supervised. By doing this, you will be mimicking the dam's reaction to rough play that occurred when your puppy was a newborn and this method continues to teach this lesson in a way that canines understand best.

 With two dogs, each should not only have their own food and water bowls, but those bowls should not be placed next to each other. While the idea of having two dogs that eat side-by-side is a cute picture in one's imagination, most of the time neither dog will be happy.

In fact, it can create a very hostile environment. To canines, food equals survival...both literally and symbolically. Dogs must have their own space and never feel as if another dog (or a human) is too close to their food. It is best for each to have his own designated eating area in opposite corners of the kitchen.

 It is rare that two dogs will agree that they are equals. All dogs, by pure raw canine instinct, know that they exist in a pack (your family). Every pack must have leader (you). Under that leadership, there will be various ranks. With two canines, one will be the Alpha (the leader dog) and one will be the Beta (the follower dog). Do not feel "sorry" for the Beta, he will be happy to know his rank and will have a wonderful sense of security that he belongs to his "pack". Dogs cannot be at ease until they know this ranking and understand their position.

Once it is settled which dog is Alpha and which is Beta, both will be content and feel secure. If this is not settled by the dogs and one does not naturally assume the position of Alpha, tension will often build. The owner will need to step in and make the decision for them.

While one may at first assume that the dog that lived the longest in the home would be the Alpha, this is not always how it will be. If one dog is male and one is female, most often the male will be Alpha (sometimes a strong female will take the role; however it is rare and usually will only happen if she was the first dog in the home and is older). In most cases of same gender dogs, the older dog will take the Alpha position regardless of which dog has lived in the home longer.

## You May Need to Step In

If there appears to be tension with both dogs vying for the Alpha position, you will need to choose the appropriate Alpha and then take steps to teach both dogs what their rank is. You can do this by using *all* of the following methods in conjunction with each other. Choosing one method alone rarely works; it is only when all methods are combined will both dogs have a clear understanding.

While these may seem like simple elements, each sends a very strong message to the dogs and when all implemented together, it is a message that a dog will rarely challenge.

 At each meal time, you will set down the Alpha's food first, allowing him or her to eat for a full 10 seconds before placing down the Beta's food. (This is a long enough time for a canine to become very aware that the Alpha is eating first, yet a short enough time that he will not work his way into a tizzy).

When giving snacks, follow this rule, however you can allow for just 5 seconds to pass.

 Whenever you leave the home with both dogs, the Alpha should leave first.

To be exact, the order should be: You, any other humans, the Alpha dog and then the Beta dog.

This applies when entering the home as well.

 Show the same amount of attention to both dogs; keeping in mind that the attention needs may be different for each pet. For example, a puppy's needs may be interactional play and an older dog's needs may be gentle petting while he sits beside you on the sofa.

## Cats and Puppies = Food Issues

For cats and dogs that live in the same household, one of the most common frustrations that owners have is that the puppy is eating the cat's food or is picking through the cat litter. This must not be allowed. While cat food is not toxic to dogs, it most certainly is not healthy. It has a completely different fat ratio as well as differences in protein and carbohydrates.

The one thing that your cat can do that your puppy cannot is reach high places, since a cat can jump and climb. Therefore, the cat's food and litter box should be placed in separate areas that your puppy cannot reach. You may choose to have them both high off of the ground. Alternatively, you can gate off a small area that the cat will be able to reach, however the gate will block your puppy from entering.

## A Happy Family Unit

Now you know to test the animals first for any signs of intolerance, how to help them decide on their ranking in the "pack" if they have not settled the matter and how to help both feel comfortable. When you show love and attention to both, in the way that each needs, you can have a multi-pet household that functions as one happy unit.

# Your Dog as a Passenger in the Car – It Needn't be a Nightmare

Not all dogs naturally enjoy riding in a car. Since most owners do need to drive to different places and since we often want (or need) to bring our dog, it can be frustrating when a puppy or dog shows signs of distress.

The distress may be due to fear...*Or* it may be a *physical* reaction to the movement of the car (motion sickness), just like some humans have.

A dog *may* have *both* a fear of the car *and* suffer from motion sickness at the same time. Therefore, these issues will be talked about separately, however an owner may need to implement coping methods for both.

Either or both issues may manifest as: shaking, drooling, whimpering, whining, barking out of control and/or vomiting.

## If Your Puppy is Afraid of the Car

Slow de-sensitization training works wonders for dogs that have a fear of riding in a car. Training works best when a dog is a puppy; however with this training method, a dog of any age can be helped. A dog that is stressed during car rides needs to have a fresh start that permits him to become used to this element in gradual way. This will allow him to gain self-confidence which will then allow him to maintain control.

Begin by simply bringing your puppy into your car when it is *not running*. If your dog hesitates to enter, offer treats to urge him to move closer. Slowly open the door, while talking in a happy and praising tone. Never force your puppy into the car; if your dog is showing signs of extreme nervousness just allow him to calm down and *then* gently urge him closer and closer with the lure of a treat.

It can be very helpful to place your dog's favorite blanket or toy inside of the car. For safety reasons, you should have your puppy secure. Small dogs do well with canine booster seats. The buckles keep your dog secure and the raised seat allows them to be high enough to see out of the window which can be a great help.

Larger dogs should be secured with a canine automobile safety harness. Crating rarely works as dogs that are confined during times of stress simply become more stressed. Even without the car not moving, you will want your dog to become used to the booster seat or automobile safety harness, so that this needn't be an additional issue as you move forward in training.

 **Having your dog in a canine booster seat or secured with a safety harness avoids the following potential mishaps and injuries:**

- **A dog on your lap or loose in the car can cause major *physical* distractions while you are driving. He can block your view, interfere with your reach of the gear shift, etc.**
- **A dog on your lap or loose in the car can cause major *mental* distractions while you are driving. Even a moment of diversion can be disastrous.**

- **A loose dog can be thrown off of a seat not only in the case of an accident, but even if a driver needs to abruptly step on the brake.**
- **A dog that sticks his head out of the window can suffer eye injuries from loose debris in the wind or even be injured by tree branches, etc.**

Once you have your dog in either his booster seat or sitting with the safety harness on, the goal will be to have short sessions of simply sitting in the car, focusing on something else.

Make this enjoyable. Bring some treats, talk in a happy and upbeat tone. Show him a new toy and encourage him to chew at it. Pet your puppy a lot and praise him. You will want to do this at random times throughout the day and spend at least 5 to 10 minutes per de-sensitization training session. Remember, this is done with the car not turned on.

After approximately 2 weeks, you should repeat the above training; *however* have the car *running*. This will allow your puppy to become accustomed to the sound of the engine, while not being subjected to the actual movement yet.

If at any time, your dog shows signs of being afraid; talk to him in a matter-of-fact, relaxed and happy way to reassure him at all is just fine (just be sure to not speak in a soothing way). The tone of your voice and your actions will be of great value. Spend at least 10 minutes, once per day. It is recommended to do this at random times, so that your puppy does not learn that it is "car time" at any one certain time of the day.

At the end of each session, have a special play time, perhaps tossing a ball or engaging in another activity that you know your puppy enjoys. This will teach him that maintaining control in the car equals some fun afterward. Play needn't be for a long time... even 5 or 10 minutes can instill the lesson that maintaining control brings about benefits.

It is now time for phase 3 of this training. With your puppy now comfortable with the harness or booster seat, the car and the noise, you can begin slow de-sensitization training for *movement*. Drive very slowly around your immediate neighborhood, avoiding full stops when at all possible. You will not want to begin by choosing a route that consists of many "stop and goes".

These sessions should begin with just a couple of minutes of driving...You can increase the time as your puppy proves himself to handle things; he may never *love* riding in the car and therefore the goal will be for him to *tolerate* it.

While you are driving, offer great words of praise. As soon as the session is complete, offer a small treat and at least 5 minutes of play time. Consistence is the key. The more you offer this very short, calm driving experience, the better your puppy will be able to slowly and steadily become accustomed to this.

In 1 to 2 weeks, the short little drives up and down your neighborhood will be increasing. By Week Two, a 10 minute drive should be the goal. Over the course of the next month or so, you will want to work up to your ultimate goal. *Your ultimate goal should be no longer than the expected driving time that your dog will need to be in the car.* For some owners who only drive around locally, this may be 15 minutes. For others who wish to bring their dog with them to visit friends in another town, this may be 30 minutes.

Great praise in a calm and happy tone should be given throughout this training. This works best if the puppy is being driven to a destination that offers some fun. This helps the puppy associate the car with receiving a benefit. Your destination can be a dog park, beach or other area that you know your puppy will love to stretch his legs, run around and enjoy a new setting.

If the *only* cause of distress was fear, if the preceding training is followed, a puppy can learn to love (or at least tolerate) a car ride. With at least one drive each month, to remind him of his lesson, he can forever behave when being driven around.

If you will be driving for more than 30 minutes, do be sure to bring water, a travel bowl for the water, snacks, a leash, toys and, if your dog is on medication, bring double just in case you are gone longer than expected.

It will be best to plan to stop and have a 5 to 10 minute break roughly halfway through the drive. This offers your dog an opportunity to go to the bathroom, to drink some water, to have a snack if he is hungry, to stretch his legs and basically have a nice respite from the ride.

If the issue is that he was not only afraid, but *also* suffering from the horrible effects of motion sickness, this is a *completely* different topic and is discussed ahead.

## Canine Car Sickness

Just like people, some dogs have motion sickness. For these dogs, it is best to limit driving only when necessary, such as needed veterinarian visits. No amount of training can stop a dog from having nausea and/or vomiting in the car when suffering from this.

However, feeding a light meal 2-3 hours before a needed car drive can help. You will certainly not want to feed your dog right before a drive. Take breaks whenever possible if you will be driving for more than 15 minutes. Even a 4 minute break given halfway through can help a dog's stomach calm down, allow him to gain a sense of footing and be "refreshed" to continue on.

You may also wish to speak with your veterinarian, as your puppy may be given a medication such as Dramamine if driving must be done; the dosing should be overseen by the veterinarian. Dramamine can be purchased over-the-counter; *however it will be different than the one prescribed by the veterinarian.* Never give your dog Dramamine that is intended for humans.

# Your Dog and Your New Baby

Your dog is probably used to being the "baby" in the home and if you are expecting a human baby, this will be a big adjustment for everyone. Some owners worry if they will need to find a new home for their dog in order to keep their baby safe....This is rarely warranted.

You will need to supervise your dog at times that he has access to the baby. Most dogs will adjust fine if socialization training begins far before the baby arrives and continues after the baby comes home. Seldom must an owner find a new home for their canine family member.

With this said, if you have a dog that has had displays of aggression, while training can be helpful it is not recommended to take any chances! The safety of your human family must come first. For owners of a breed that is known for having a low tolerance toward children or any dog that has been proven to have an aggressive temperament, re-homing your dog may be necessary.

However, for all other dog owners, by implementing training both before and after your new arrival, everything can run very smoothly. Usually, those who have issues with the interaction between their dog and their baby are those who did not plan ahead of time.

As soon as you learn that you will be expecting a baby, training should begin for your dog; this will ensure that your dog has plenty of time to become accustomed to the anticipated changes. Some of the changes will be: The layout of the home, those wonderful new scents of a baby and your dog's schedule (as you may need to rearrange daily activities around the new baby).

## Basic Commands

Things will run much smoother if your dog understands and always listens to basic commands. You will want your dog to immediately: Sit, Stay and Heel on command. If your dog has not yet mastered these commands, begin training right away.

# Before Your Baby Arrives

Due to the fact the a baby's immune system is not strong, ensure that your dog is healthy and is up to date with de-wormings and vaccinations before the baby arrives.

There is much to help your dog become accustomed to, so it is best to begin training well in advance. You can help your dog become used to the scents of your new baby by taking some baby powder and rubbing it into the carpeting, soft wash cloths etc. and allowing your dog to become very familiar with the scent. Just be sure to rub it into a soft fabric first and not allow your dog to play with the actual container.

If you have a baby mobile or other baby toys that make noise, it will help to sit down with your dog on a regular basis to hear those noises. With months of hearing twinkling baby songs, this sound will not be surprising at all once your baby arrives.

If you believe that you will be changing the layout of your home, do this as soon as possible. Dogs do best when given consistency. If a baby highchair is going to be in the spot where his food once was and his food is going to be moved to another corner in the kitchen, make this change now.

If your dog balks at the idea of having his food moved and you absolutely *must* change the location of his dishes, you can do this slowly. Each day you can move the food dish and water bowl a few inches. After a while, you will reach your goal.

One of the biggest changes that a dog will endure is the ongoing sound of the baby's cries. When dogs have a few months to become *gradually* accustomed to this element, this is proven to help reduce stress and/or anxiety that a dog would otherwise feel. This is especially true for shy, nervous dogs or overprotective dogs.

If a neighbor, friend or family member has a baby, it is recommended to ask permission to record the baby's noises for a while. Most babies will let out various cries during a recording session. You can then play this section of the recording for your dog.

This is such a great help when a dog can be desensitized to the sounds over a period of time instead of being "bombarded" with them all of a sudden.

When you begin, listening sessions should be short (five minutes at the most) and with the volume on a very quiet setting. It is best to sit down with your dog so that you can help direct his focus on the recording at this early stage. Talk in a very matter-of-fact tone of voice. You will *not* want to offer soothing words, as a dog can assume that this means that you are confirming that he has something to be concerned about.

Any time that your dog stays calm during a session, reward with praise and a treat. As with all training, do be sure that the treat is not one that would normally be given as a snack.

As your dog becomes used to the noise, increase the time spent listening, in increments of five minutes at first, and then increments of ten minutes after a couple of weeks. Volume should increase as well until you reach the point of being able to play the recording at the natural volume.

Do not underestimate the volume of a crying baby, as it can be quite loud. Usually, only with this method of gradual desensitization will a dog be able to tolerate such a piercing, continual noise.

**Fact** A decibel (dB) is the unit used to measure how loud a sound is. The smallest audible sound is 0 dB... very loud noises such as a shotgun measure 170 dB. To give you an idea of just how loud a baby's cry can be, let's look at the following:

**The hum of an air conditioner is 50 to 75 dB. An alarm clock ranges between 65 to 80 dB. Car horns, motorcycles and baby cries all average 110 dB, just a bit lower than an ambulance siren of 120 dB.**

Once you are at the *fifteen minute mark and beyond,* while the recording is playing, encourage your dog to focus on a particular task. Best is to play with a favorite toy. You will want it to be an *independent* task; if you choose to play fetch, this would not work well as he would expect that interaction with you in the future while you will be tending to the baby.

If he chews on the toy, offer praise, and at the end of the session, offer a treat. Doing this, he will learn that: crying sounds = find a toy and play = you are happy and he receives attention and a treat.

If you reach a length of time or a level of volume that causes your dog to show signs of discomfort, stop the session and urge him to direct his focus on something else. Do not offer praise but also do not reprimand. His discomfort will be your signal that the next session should be shorter and your dog needs more desensitizing to the sounds before moving to a more intense level.

Some dogs simply cannot handle extended crying noises, this is especially true for older dogs that spend their time resting and not playing with toys. After implementing this training, if you find that your dog has limited or zero tolerance for the crying noises you will want to offer a different solution. If a dog does not have the *capability* to learn tolerance, it cannot be forced. Therefore, as an alternative, it is suggested to offer your dog an area where he can retreat to.

A dog bed or opened crate filled with soft baby blankets placed in a quiet corner and a favorite chew can help a dog to find a certain level of relief. Making this a designated area to retreat to offers a dog a plan…He will learn that during an episode of crying that he has the choice of heading to a specific comfortable location, removing himself from the immediate area as opposed to remaining close by.

This area should not be enclosed. When a dog is anxious, this feeling often increases if he is confined. Also, your dog should know that he has the option of leaving this area whenever he wishes.

In this case, you will want to continue with the recording sessions, however when your dog shows distress, you will encourage him to head to the designated area. Do not offer soothing words, as a dog can interpret this as your confirmation that the cries are an irritant. Speak in a matter-of-fact voice when leading him there. You will be acknowledging his validity to need to retreat without encouraging intolerance. Any time that your dog does not bark or display any other negative behavior while the recording is playing, offer praise. Once a session is done, offer praise and a treat.

Before bringing your baby home from the hospital, send home a blanket or gown that the baby has been wrapped in. This will allow your dog to become used to your baby's particular scent.

## Your Baby's Toys and Your Dog's Toys

If baby toys are in reach of your dog, he will have no idea of the difference between those toys and his own unless you teach this to him. It is best to choose a designated area for your dog's toys and if possible, a designated area for your baby's toys.

It will be important to show your dog which toys he is allowed to play with and which he is not allowed to touch. This is very important; as you would not want your dog thinking that the baby is playing with "his" toy which can cause a dog to mouth it from the baby's hands.

Any time that your dog trots over to the baby's toys, distract him by clapping your hands together or by calling out his name. Choose the method that is most effective. As soon as you have his attention, urge him to play with one of his favorite chew toys.

If he does indeed follow your lead, offer praise. If two full minutes pass by and he is still focused on his own toy, offer a treat. Done in this way, you are not reprimanding your dog for being curious, but you are distracting him and then showing what is appropriate to play with.


## Only a Certain Amount of Time

Even the best parents in the world (of both babies and dogs) cannot be in two places at once. With the arrival of a baby, there will be times when your dog cannot receive the same amount of attention that he was once used to.

It is best to make this change before the arrival of the baby and not afterward when your dog may become jealous.  If the main caretaker of your dog is going to be the main caretaker of the baby, another household member should start to be included in the care of your dog.  This includes taking the dog for walks, feeding him, grooming him, etc.

It can be done as shared tasks at first, with two people taking the dog for walks, etc. After a week or so, alternate this by having it be a shared task one day and have only the new designated dog walker/ feeder/ bather, etc. be in full charge the next.

It will be important for your dog to follow commands just as he did earlier. A well-trained dog will obey commands given from every human in the home who was involved with training.

Two owners *can* share the tasks just about all of the time, however there must be *some* days when *only* the new "care-giver" is in charge since the need for this will inevitably occur once the baby arrives.

Done in slow, steady steps, this will allow your dog plenty of time to become used to receiving care from a different human family member.

## After the Baby Arrives

Associate the baby's presence with positive things. Give your dog attention and praise for desired behavior around the baby. Randomly, also offer a treat. Do not place the baby on the floor with the dog unless someone is right there to supervise.

Never yell or reprimand your dog for approaching your baby incorrectly. Instead, gently show your dog what you wish for him to do and offer a reward for responding.

## Jealousy

Even with very careful planning, months in advance, some dogs may be a bit jealous or become "clingy" to you once the baby is home. It is best to continue on with your planned schedule and follow the guidelines that we have discussed. If your dog is extremely clingy, do acknowledge him by giving a quick pat and then do what you must to care for your baby.

If you are sitting on the sofa feeding your baby, you can also have your dog close to you to cuddle. When you take the baby for a walk in the stroller, you can take your dog along as well.  In time, your dog will become used to having a little brother or sister.

# Thunderstorm Training

Many dogs are afraid of thunderstorms, yet often canines *do* have a *valid* reason for showing discomfort during this type of weather.

Some dogs could have a hurricane blow in around them and they would remain calm, chewing on their favorite toy. However, the majority of dogs have a heightened sense of awareness during storms. And a percentage of those dogs become very alarmed during thunderstorms.

Some people talk of this issue as if it is a canine phobia. However, *unlike* most phobias that are based on an *imagined* fear, a dog has very good reasons to be afraid of thunder.

All dogs have their own personalities, however most dogs that are truly frightened of thunder will do one or all of the following: Attempt to hide, shake, whine, pace back and forth, begin to drool excessively, bark out of control, and/or chew items that they normally would not, such as furniture.

In *severe* cases a dog *may* simply lose all control, some have been known to run into doors, break windows, etc.

If your dog behaves this way toward thunder, it is time to step in and help him gain control over his actions and reactions. It is important to look at this from your dog's point of view. There are 5 main elements that may cause a dog to behave frantically during a storm:

*The flashes of light* – This can be quite disturbing to a dog and cause him to lose his feeling of security and control over his normal environment.

*The noise of the thunder* – This is loud for you and I...can you imagine how this sounds to a dog whose hearing is much more sensitive than a human's?

The frequencies that dogs pick up are more than twice the range of our capabilities and they can detect sounds from as far away as four times the distance that we can.

Some studies suggest that canines can actually experience *physical* pain if thunder is loud enough.

*High winds* - Thunderstorms sometimes produce high pitched sounds that only your dog will hear and it can cause him to panic.

 *The sound of the rain hitting the roof of your home* – With a dog's heightened sense of hearing, the continual pounding of rain can be quite irritating.

 *The air pressure* – Surely you know of that "feeling" you get when a storm is on its way. You can actually "sense" when a storm is coming, you "feel it in the air". Your dog, with heightened senses, feels this hundreds of times stronger than you do.

 In the United States, Florida has the most thunderstorms per year of any other state. Louisiana, Mississippi, Alabama and Georgia follow as the next top four. The "Safest Lightening" states are Washington State, Oregon, California, Idaho and Maine.

# Is This Normal Behavior?

Studies are interesting on this subject. It is suggested that some dog breeds are more prone to behave negatively to storms than other breeds. While any dog of any breed may be sensitive to thunder, dogs in the Herding, Sporting and Working families are found to be more apt to show this behavior.

Why? It is suggested that these dog breeds have been taught over centuries to be *very* aware of their immediate environment. *At the same time,* the trait of suppressing aggressiveness was bred in; thus causing them to react with anxiety instead.

Rescue puppies and dogs are more likely to be afraid of thunder. Many rescues have a lack of socialization skills that would otherwise aid in helping them to maintain control. Most have also experienced many unpleasant things before being rescued which may simply make them more skittish in many situations.

# How to Help

The training technique of desensitization usually works very well, although it cannot take away any *physical* pain that a dog may experience due to loud thunder or air pressure changes. For dogs with extreme fear, this type of training will at least help calm them down enough that they will be able to cope better.

The theory of this type of dog training is to slowly allow your dog to become used to the noises and lights. The change in air pressure will be addressed after a dog is more comfortable with these two elements.

It is suggested to purchase a CD recording of thunderstorms. These can be found at just about any CD store and are usually used to help people sleep.

It is important to remember that success cannot be found overnight. This type of training is a step-by-step process. You will need to remain consistent in your efforts while taking things slowly.

You will want to choose a time in the day when your dog is at peace, such as after a walk when he is resting and comfortable. Sit on the floor, patting your dog gently, and allow the CD to play at a very low volume.

If your dog's ears perk up or if he appears restless, reassure him with gentle, calming words and continue to pat him. Soothing words *are* allowed for this type of training (unlike many others) since a dog has legitimate reasons for his fear.

Allow the sounds to play for about 5 minutes on the first day.

*Week 1:* Keep the volume of the CD the same, however increase the time by 1 minute each day until your dog can sit through approximately 15 minutes of very soft thunder noises and remain calm.

*Week 2:* Repeat the training of week 1, however now you will have a helper flicker the lights in the home on and off at random times while the noises of the thunder plays softly. Again, patting your dog and reassuring him that everything is okay with your gentle and calm voice.

*Week 3:* Continue this training each day for the 15 minutes. However, every other day, slightly increase the volume of the thunder sounds. It will be your calm actions and your gentle, reassuring words that will show your dog that all is fine and that thunder is a temporary element.

Since most thunderstorms are fleeting, the most amount of time that a dog needs to become used to the sounds are the 15 minute mark. Any time that a dog completes a session while remaining calm, great praise and a treat should be given.

## Air Pressure

The only way to train your dog to stay calm when the air pressure changes, is *during* a thunderstorm. When one does occurs, you should remain very calm. Your motions should never be rushed. Some owners will run over to windows to slam them shut or run across the room to close a door. Try to avoid any of those types of actions: your dog may interpret them as your confirmation that there is an approaching danger.

While the storm is taking place, pat your dog and talk calmly just as you did during the training exercises. If he shows *effort* to remain calm, do offer calm attention, praise and a treat. While you cannot eliminate the legitimate, physical reasons for this anxiety, you can offer reward when a dog tries to maintain control while experiencing it.

# If Your Dog Does Not Respond to Training

Most dogs will respond very well to this training, however some dogs are simply too sensitive to the noises and air pressure changes for training to work enough for them to remain calm.

Some veterinarians suggest giving a mild anti-anxiety medication to dogs. However, you may want to rethink this *unless* you live in an area that receives substantial thunderstorms. Why? Because most thunderstorms only last for a very brief period of time and do not happen that often. It will be done in vain to offer medical sedation to a dog when the storm will be gone by the time the medication begins to work.

As an alternative, just as with possible intolerance to a baby's cries, it is suggested to offer your dog an area where he can retreat to. A dog bed or crate filled with soft baby blankets and a favorite toy can help a dog to find some level of comfort. Making this a *designated* area to retreat to offers a dog a plan...He will learn that during a thunderstorm he has a *specific* comfortable area to "wait it out" as opposed to running around frantically.

*This area should not be enclosed.* When a dog is scared, he can panic even more if he is confined. Your dog should know that he has the option of leaving this area as soon as he wishes to.

Remember that your actions and tone of voice mean a lot. Showing your dog that a storm does not affect *you* at all will help him to understand that no danger is present and that the event, while uncomfortable, is temporary.

# Exploring and Expanding Your Dog's World

Now that you know all of the essentials of proper socialization and have taken the time to work with your puppy to provide proper training, you may want to think about how to keep your puppy or dog engaged in the world and all that it offers.

While some dogs may be perfectly happy staying at home most of the time, many will thrive when introduced to new things.

You will never know just how much your dog will enjoy a certain activity unless you offer him an opportunity to experience it. You may find that your life is expanded as well, as both of you may find something to be pleasurable enough to do it on a regular basis.

## Places to Ponder

Here are some places that you may want to think about exploring with your dog:

**The beach:** If you live within driving distance to a beach, this can be a wonderful place to walk with your dog. Most dogs love walking along the water. It is suggested to do socialization in regard to both people and animals before heading out to a crowded beach. Once your dog is familiar with the concept of proper behavior during Meet and Greets, the beach can be an engaging and fun location. Many dogs enjoy this setting and you may find strolling along the shoreline to be very relaxing.

Many people only think about the beach during the summertime; however it can be quite enjoyable during all seasons including winter (when both dog and owner are properly bundled up).

Do be aware that grains of sand can be a strange feeling for a puppy that has never walked upon this surface. It may take a few outings before your dog is used to the sensation of walking upon this surface.

**A Lake or Pond:** Those who may not have easy access to the shoreline of an ocean may often have access to a lake or pond. Depending on where you live, this can offer a many great experiences. Some lakes will be a perfect location to watch ducks and swans drift by and hear the laughter of children as they throw bread crumbs.

Some ponds can be a great place to explore...You may need to dress with appropriate boots for the mud, but can find yourself smiling as you and your dog discover frogs and turtles. You can bring a picnic lunch and both enjoy the sunshine and fresh air.

**The Park:** Many owners wish that they lived near a dog park; however many parks do allow dogs, that fact may just not be advertised. One of my favorite parks to take walks has the smallest sign that one could imagine, with faded printing that states, "Dogs must be on leash". While it is not an "official" dog park and many people are there without their pets, it is a perfect place to ponder nature, toss a ball in one of the enclosed softball areas and sit down to people watch.

**Trails:** Many owners hear about the suggestion to go on "hiking trails" with their dog for fun and adventure but wonder where in the world these trails are that their dog can actually maneuver. You may have better luck with "walking trails".

One of my favorite trails to take a walk through actually runs around a large hospital. While the trees that surround the hospital appear to be just that: Trees....Behind those trees there is actually a path that winds in a big circle, allowing you to exit right near where you park your car to enter. So, keep this in mind and do an internet search for walking trails as well as hiking trails.

**Children's Softball Games:** At the beginning of this book, we discussed the tiny Pomeranian that I had rescued when she was approximately ten years old. We talked about how she had never before had known what grass beneath her paws felt like. As she began to be socialized to the world, it was discovered that she loved coming along to watch my sons play softball. She enjoyed the overall happy vibes of the crowd and loved to stretch her legs during walks that we would take to the snack stand and for her bathroom breaks.

My sons are long since grown and no longer play softball on gorgeous spring and summer evenings....but this location is still a perfect place to enjoy spending time with a dog. You do not need to be a mother of softball playing children to be a spectator at a local game!

This offers a great place for different activities. Your puppy can Meet and Greet with children, he can enjoy being held in the stands and will be intrigued by the balls flying around. He can be taken for walks...either quieter ones around the outside of the fields or busier ones to the snack stands.

**The Pet Store:** One of the great things about local pet supply stores is that many happily welcome pets to go inside. You will of course need to have first socialized your puppy for other dogs and for people. You will want to be careful not to buy expensive things every time you go; but it can be fun to meet other owners and enjoy seeing what is new every now and then.

**Outdoor Malls:** While security may quickly escort you and your dog out of Macy's if you try to bring him into an indoor mall with you….There are often no laws at all in regard to outdoor malls. Many will have outdoor eating patios outside of food establishments (where you can sip on an inexpensive juice or water) and you can stroll around and window shop.

**Outdoor Craft Shows/ Art Shows/ Fairs/ Festivals/ Yard Sales:** Keep an eye out for advertisements and flyers for any outdoor activities that may be coming around to your area.

While these are normally warm weather events, many towns hold winter events as well such as ice sculpture contests and tree lightings. Keep your options open; this is especially fun for those who are single and may not often venture out on their own...With your puppy with you, you always have a companion for these types of events and you will never feel alone.

## There is No Limit

We are so used to our world, we often forget (or simply cannot remember) that everything was once new to us as well. There was a first encounter with every element that now exists in our world around us as we know it.

No matter what the size of your world, try to slowly and gradually allow your dog's world to be as big as possible. You can both enjoy expanding worlds as a team. Every experience is an opportunity to learn. Every time that a dog is lovingly shown a new situation (lake, beach, walking trail, craft show, etc.) and he becomes familiarized to it, it then becomes a new opportunity for you to bond with your dog and enjoy settings and situations as a team.

Unless a location specially bars dogs and/or pets, always keep your eyes open for a new place to explore. You may find a new location once a year, but meanwhile you and your dog may have several favorite spots that you frequent on a regular basis.

Each time that you take your dog to an environment outside of the home, even if it is the same "favorite hangout", you are expanding his world. There will be different people walking by, different dogs, a different feel to the air depending on the season, different distractions and more.

Remember that even if something is not of particular interest to you, if your puppy has never seen it before or has never noticed it before, he may just wish to discover it. It may be worth staying outside for a few extra minutes if it allows your puppy to see, discover and learn about a squirrel's activities or hear and then learn to tolerate the noise of your neighbor's lawnmower.

It can be entertainingly beneficial to spend a few extra moments at the kitchen sink if you notice that your puppy is having fun pawing at the tiny bubbles floating down toward him...Or to spend some time outside after shoveling the fallout after a snowstorm to allow your puppy to become familiar with and then play in the snow for a little while.

Your dog's mind is capable of holding a great deal of information. Studies have proven that dogs feel complex emotions and are capable of understanding upward of two hundred words. Your dog is a very intelligent animal. It is your job to teach him that there needn't be fear of anything that you deem to be safe. As your dog's leader, lead him to be a self-confident and happy dog.

**Other books by Faye Dunningham**

(Found on Amazon!)

The Well Trained Puppy:
Housebreaking, Commands to Shape Behavior and
All Training Needed for a Happy, Obedient Dog


Chewing, Tugging, Nipping and Biting:
Detailed Step-by-Step Training for Puppies and Dogs

Made in the USA
San Bernardino, CA
01 September 2017